THREADS

20 Hand Embroidery Designs to Enhance Your Clothes

Madeleine Kemsley

THREADS

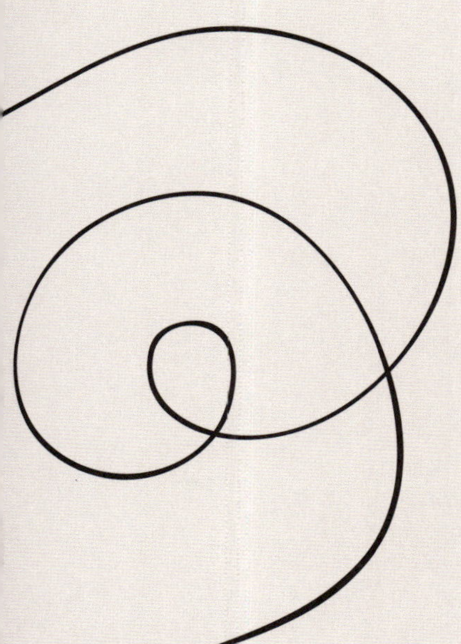

20 Hand Embroidery Designs to Enhance Your Clothes

Madeleine Kemsley

Photography by Amelia Pemberton

Quadrille

CONTENTS

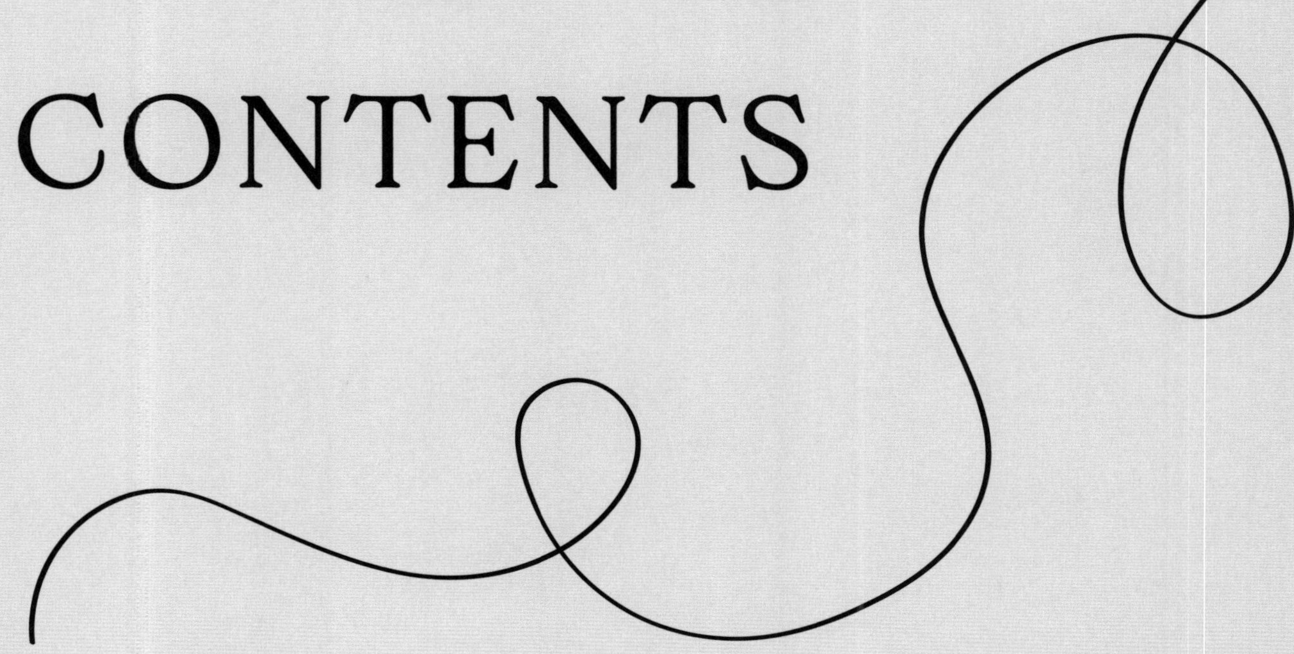

HOW TO USE THIS BOOK

***Threads* is designed to help and inspire you to embroider your own clothing with beautiful motifs based on folk art and the natural world. The book contains eight step-by-step projects and within each project are instructions on how to apply 20 original embroidery designs to a range of different garments.**

To get started, I recommend exploring the Stitch Guide (see page 24) first. This section will introduce you to all the embroidery techniques used throughout the projects. You'll also learn how to create a stitch sampler on which you can practise and refine your skills before starting on a garment.

Once you're comfortable with the stitch techniques, you can take a look at the information on Choosing a Garment (see page 20). Here, you'll find guidance on choosing the ideal garments for embroidery and selecting fabrics with the right properties for your project.

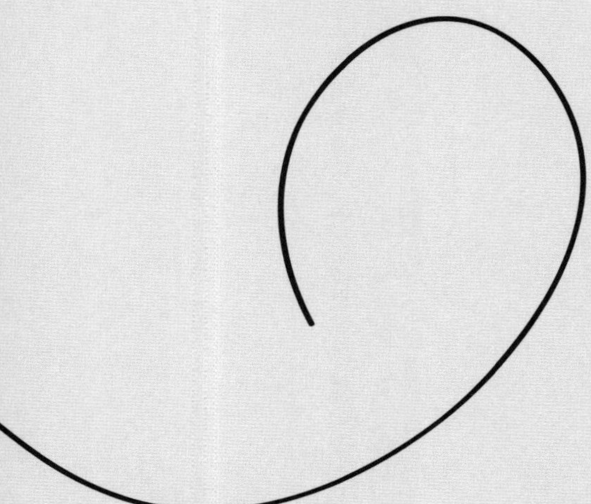

Once you've sourced a garment, it's time to pick a design project. Each project can be adapted for different types of clothing. While some designs work best with specific features – such as on a collared shirt or pockets – you can easily modify any design to suit your chosen garment.

PROJECT INSTRUCTIONS

Each project follows a consistent format to make the process simple and enjoyable.

1. **Design Reference:** A line drawing of the design is available to guide you. Use it to sketch directly onto the fabric with a vanishing marker or, if freehand drawing isn't for you, download a PDF version (see page 135) to print and trace using a light box or use the transfer method described on page 19.

2. **Thread Suggestions:** Each motif features a list of the thread colours I used for the design. Feel free to follow my palette or select your own to suit your personal style.

3. **Step-by-Step Guidance:** The instructions detail which stitches to use for each part of the design, and in which order, making it easy to follow along.

ENJOY YOUR NEW CRAFT

One of the beautiful things about embroidery is that it doesn't require much equipment, so you can take your project anywhere. Whether you're curled up by the fire or sitting under the dappled shade of a tree, make some time for slowness and enjoy the process.

LIFE IN CORNWALL

I've been in Cornwall for the past 10 years, mostly living in a caravan on a farm just outside Falmouth. Over this time, I've developed a deep attachment to my life here.

Although it's not always easy, there's something undeniably special about living in Cornwall. I'm fortunate to be surrounded by lots of resourceful and creative people who live in alternative ways. There's less pressure to follow the traditional pipeline of working a potentially unfulfilling job and settling down, which creates a greater sense of possibility for what life can be. Along with that, there's a strong sense of community here that I haven't found elsewhere, with a network of friends spanning various age groups. Whenever I leave Cornwall, I feel like I'm stepping into 'the real world' after spending time in this special little microcosm.

I'm well placed here to explore my love of shape and colour as Cornwall has such a wide variety of landscapes, from misty, muddy creeks to mauve, heather-covered cliffs above the sea. I spend most of my time in the verdant, sheltered areas around the Helford River. The unique microclimate here gives it a subtropical feel, with prehistoric plants like giant ferns and gunneras flourishing. Occasionally, I venture over to the equally beautiful north coast, which offers a stark contrast with its windswept, shrub-covered landscapes and good vantage points to watch the sunset.

Nature has a significant influence on my work, with many of my motifs derived from flora and fauna. I've always been massively inspired by different types of folk art, a lot of which originates from communities deeply connected to nature, whether they rely on it for their livelihood or live in remote areas, resulting in a profound respect for the environment. While not all my designs are directly linked to the plants and animals of Cornwall, living in such a beautiful and slow-paced place has deepened my connection to this tactile craft. This connection between the landscape and craft is the reason I chose to photograph all my pieces outside.

The folk art that inspires me includes a wide range of styles, from the simple, figurative elements often seen in American quilts to the bold, colourful paintings from cultures within Eastern Europe. What has always captivated me is the simplistic nature of much of this art. It's the kind of work that feels unpolished, yet full of vibrancy and creativity. I've always been particularly drawn to folk art that embodies this playful, unrefined quality. It's the simplicity of the shapes, often balanced with an innate sense of symmetry, that speaks to me. Much of my own work is influenced by this sense of innocence and directness, incorporating these naïve forms to create compositions that feel both grounded and harmonious, yet full of life and energy.

I first started embroidery during a particularly anxious time in my life, and it has since become a great outlet as it's a wonderful practice for mindfulness. On dry, windless days, I love stitching outdoors. Embroidery is such a portable craft and requires minimal equipment, making it perfect for taking anywhere. In the summer, I can often be found sitting on a blanket in the long grass, stitching away, and in the winter, I retreat to my studio or sit in front of the wood burner in my caravan to work on my projects.

GETTING

STARTED

TOOLS OF THE TRADE

In this section I introduce you to the equipment you will need to complete the projects in this book and how to use it. As well as helping you identify what tools you will need to try your hand at the projects, this section will also give you an insight into the decision-making process behind the creation of the designs.

There are four main aspects to consider when planning a piece: choosing your embroidery hoop, finding the appropriate threads, selecting needles, and deciding on what design transfer method is best for you.

The recommendations outlined here are based on my own experience: I am a self-taught embroiderer, so they are comprised of my personal experience of what works best for this specific style of embroidery rather than a general statement on what embroidery tools are best. Feel free to experiment and see what works for you.

CHOOSING YOUR EMBROIDERY HOOP

The purpose of an embroidery hoop is to create tension in the fabric, which allows the needle to penetrate more precisely and prevents stitches from bunching. The main thing to consider when choosing an embroidery hoop is the size. There are pros and cons to both big and small sizes but to be able to create all the projects in this book, you will probably need to choose both a mid-size and a small hoop. Big hoops enable you to cover a larger area of fabric, so you don't have to move your work as often. This can be good for a large design; however, larger hoops don't hold tension as well as their smaller counterparts, so a compromise is sometimes necessary. Smaller hoops also allow you to embroider near the edges of the fabric. This is useful for areas near seams, like collars, shoulders and button plackets. A downside of smaller hoops can be that they hold too much tension and this can damage or pucker the fabric.

Embroidery hoops are available in different diameters For the projects in this book, I would recommend the following two sizes:

- Approx. 18cm (7in) This is my preferred hoop size when embroidering clothing. I used this hoop size for most of the projects in this book.
- Approx. 11.5cm (4½in) This smaller hoop is useful for finishing off any areas that are close to the edge of the fabric or if you want to embroider hard-to-reach areas near a collar or seam.

USING YOUR EMBROIDERY HOOP

The hoop consists of two parts, the inner hoop and the outer hoop. The inner hoop is a fixed ring, whereas the outer hoop can be enlarged and compressed using a screw adjustment. Start by separating the two hoops. Place the inner hoop beneath the area of fabric you want to embroider – it's easiest to do this on a flat surface. Then, take your outer hoop and push it over the inner hoop with the fabric sandwiched in between. If the outer hoop won't go on or if there is too much resistance, then enlarge it by unwinding the screw (anticlockwise). Once the fabric is in the hoop, pull the fabric evenly around the edges until it is taut like a drum. Make sure you are happy with how your transferred design looks in the hoop and are satisfied that it is not distorted. Once this is all done, tighten the screw (clockwise) to keep everything in place. As you work on the embroidery piece, the tension of the fabric may loosen and you might have to repeat the process to tauten the fabric to maintain a consistent tension.

EMBROIDERY THREADS

There are many different varieties of embroidery thread available, and the choice of thread can significantly influence the final results of your work. In this book, I used six-strand cotton threads for all the projects.

A six-strand thread comes in a skein and consists of one larger strand made up of six smaller threads. These strands can be separated to achieve the desired thickness of thread. For each of the projects in this book, I used a six-strand thread, split into three strands.

Splitting the Threads
After cutting the six-strand thread to length, use your thumbs to gently separate the end into two sections (three strands each). Place your thumb between the two sections with one hand and gently pull it along the length of the thread, keeping the tension with your other hand. Continue until you have two separate lengths of three-strand thread. Coil up one half for later use and use the other half to thread your needle.

Knotting the Thread Before You Begin
Once I've separated the thread and threaded it onto the needle, I knot the ends together at the bottom to create a loop. This ensures the thread stays securely in place and doesn't slip off the needle. This makes it much easier to embroider and helps maintain tension when stitching, without worrying about the needle coming off the thread or that your embroidery will unravel.

There are a few different ways to create a knot at the end of the thread. The method I've always used is simply tying a knot at the end by holding both sections of the thread together, forming a small loop, and then passing the end through it to create a single knot. I will usually repeat this process in the same spot to double the size of the knot, just to make sure it's big enough not to slip through the weave of the fabric.

Another common method used by many embroiderers is to loop the thread around the needle a few times, then pull the loops down the length of thread to the end to form a knot. This technique is quite similar to the process for making a French knot – which is a stitch explained in the Stitch Guide (see page 24).

Knotting the Finished Thread
Every time you change colour or reach the end of a piece of thread, you'll need to knot off to keep your stitching secure. I also recommend knotting off your thread if you're moving on to a different section of your embroidery that's quite far from where you've just been stitching – this is to avoid long lines of thread spanning the back of your fabric.

There are a few ways to knot off. The method I use most often is as follows: once you've finished the section you're working on (or are running out of thread), bring your needle to the underside of the fabric. Then, pass your needle under the last stitch you made, create a small loop, and pull the needle through it. Pull the thread taut to form a knot. I usually repeat this step twice to make it extra secure – securing stitches is especially important when embroidering clothing, as it gets more wear and tear than other embroidered artworks.

If there isn't a nearby stitch to anchor your knot, you can also use the following method: bring your needle to the underside of the design, and near the base of the thread (close to the fabric), create a small loop and pass the needle through it to form a knot.

Knotting Tips
Always leave a few inches of thread when you're coming to the end of stitching, so you have enough thread to tie a secure knot. If you stitch too close to the end, it can be tricky to knot off properly.

You don't need to knot off after every small section. If you're able to move on to another nearby area using the same colour, that's great and will save you some time. However, I recommend avoiding jumps longer than about 4cm (1½in) – anything more can leave long strands of thread on the back of the fabric – these can get caught or show through on lighter fabrics. For example, if you're filling an area with lots of French knots, you can easily move from stitch to stitch without knotting off each time. But if you're moving to a different part of the design, it's best to knot off and restart. This keeps the back of the work tidy and helps avoid unnecessary tangling or bulk.

Things To Consider When Preparing Embroidery Thread
When measuring the thread, remember that you'll be folding it over on the needle to form a loop, so you need to cut it to double the length you want to use. A longer length of thread means you'll have to re-thread the needle less often, but it can also increase the likelihood of tangling, which can be frustrating. As a

general guideline, I recommend measuring out about 2m (2⅕yd) of thread at a time. As you gain experience, you'll get a feel for how much thread you need for different sections and stitches.

The two main brands of six-strand cotton embroidery thread are DMC and Anchor. For the projects in this book I have used a selection of both brands. I have also listed all the colours I used and provided the relevant colour codes. In the resources section I have provided information on finding a colour conversion chart for the two brands. This is to make it easy for you to access the correct colours from either brand, as most haberdasheries only stock one or the other.

EMBROIDERY NEEDLES

The type of needle you use for embroidery largely depends on the style of stitching you are doing. For the techniques featured in this book, I recommend using sharp, thin needles with a narrow eye. Sharp needles allow for more precise stitches, while narrow eye holes are particularly useful for stitches like French knots. Additionally, these needles leave less of a mark on the fabric.

A good rule of thumb is that the thread should pass through the eye of the needle comfortably, but with no visible excess space around the thread. I suggest using crewel work needles or chenille needles – both have sharp tips and long eyes, making them easy to thread, but without being overly wide.

Avoid using blunt or bulky needles, such as those used for needlepoint or cross-stitch, as these can require more effort to pierce the fabric and may disrupt your stitching.

Most haberdasheries sell needles in packs containing various sizes; experimenting with one of these packs is a great way to figure out which needle is right for your project. Test out the different sizes with your chosen thread and fabric; the ideal needle should glide through the fabric with minimal resistance, without causing any damage or strain.

DESIGN TRANSFER PENS AND CARBON PAPER

When I'm creating my designs, I typically use a water-soluble pen to draw directly onto the fabric. This is a simple and effective method for transferring a design to a garment. If you sketch out a design and aren't quite happy with it, you can easily remove the pen marks by dabbing them with a wet cloth – the ink will completely disappear. Once the fabric is dry, you can redraw your design.

Once I'm satisfied with my design, I begin the embroidery process. After completing the embroidery, I simply dab away any remaining pen marks or wash the garment to fully remove them.

For the projects in this book, I'll present a variety of transfer options, as I understand that not everyone is comfortable with freehand drawing. Each project features a line drawing of the finished design and you can either copy the design directly, drawing freehand by looking at the image in the book and using a water-soluble marker, or you can choose from a selection of printable PDFs (see page 135). The PDFs can be printed at your desired size, and you can trace directly from the printout. If your fabric is light enough in colour and weight, you can use a light box or simply hold it up to a window, so the lines are visible through the fabric. Alternatively, you can use carbon fabric transfer paper placed between the printout and the fabric to trace the design. This method works especially well for transferring onto darker fabrics, as the carbon transfer paper comes in light and dark colours. See page 135 for instructions on how to do this.

CHOOSING A GARMENT

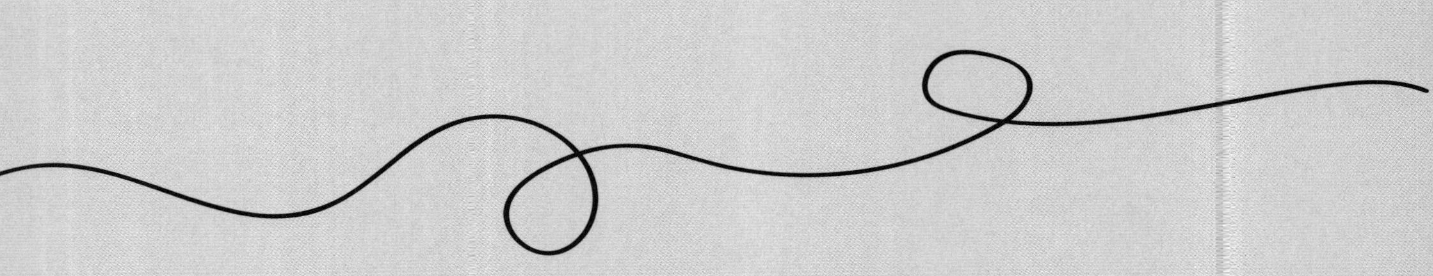

In this section, I discuss the types of garments that are appropriate for the projects in this book and where to find them. Embroidery is great for bringing new life to old garments that would otherwise end up in landfill.

Using the simple techniques outlined in this book, you can re-energize old clothes, add your own style to otherwise unadorned pieces or even cover up stains and/or repairs that have tarnished an old favourite.

WHERE TO FIND GARMENTS?

The best place to start is at home! Reworking something that you already own is the most sustainable option. Perhaps there is an item in your wardrobe you no longer reach for that could benefit from restyling? Or you may have an old favourite piece that has become marked or torn and needs some love to extend its life? Embroidery can be a great form of visible mending.

If you can't find anything appropriate at home, the next best option is to source secondhand clothing. This is both financially and ecologically sustainable. Some of my favourite places to find secondhand clothing are:

- Charity shops
- Car boot sales
- Flea markets
- Clothing swaps

If you find these places hard to access, you can also look online on sites such as eBay, Depop or Vinted to name just a few. You may also be able to use social media to connect with people interested in swapping or donating clothes.

FAVOURABLE FABRIC PROPERTIES

Ideally, you should choose fabrics with hard-wearing natural fibres, such as linen or cottons like denim and canvas. These fabrics provide a consistent medium to embroider on. As well as using natural fibres, heavyweight fabric with a tight weave is preferable. A fabric with all these properties will provide a sturdy base that is easy to work with.

FABRIC PROPERTIES TO AVOID

Materials like polyester, elastic and nylon should be avoided; characteristically, they are stretchy and slippery which makes them very difficult to work with. Their elasticity makes it challenging to maintain a consistent tension in the hoop which can lead to bunching and distortion. Fine or slippery fabric makes it tricky to be precise, is time-consuming to work with and makes it almost impossible to get a clean, consistent finish.

DRAPE

A key factor to consider when choosing your garments is the way the fabric hangs or sits on your body. Items that don't fall flat or have lots of pleats may not display your embroidery well. A good way to test this is to mark out your design with a transfer pen, try on the piece and observe in a mirror whether the drape of the garment is compatible with your design.

CARE GUIDE

Once you have finished embroidering your garments you will need to take care of them to ensure their longevity. There are things you can do to help protect them and to prolong their life.

- Handwash the item(s) in lukewarm water using a mild detergent – make sure it doesn't contain any bleach.
- Wash inside out to protect the embroidery.
- Hang to dry and do not use a tumble dryer.
- Iron if desired.
- Always check the care label of the original garment in case it requires specialist care.

STITCH GUIDE

There are hundreds of embroidery stitches out there, but I prefer to keep things simple by sticking to just five core stitches. In this guide, I'll introduce you to my five favourite stitches – which are all you need to complete any project in this book. The stitches are split stitch, satin stitch, French knots, blanket stitch and weave stitch.

For all the projects and stitches, I use three stands of cotton embroidery thread doubled over the needle and knotted together at the end. See Tools of the Trade (page 18) for instructions on how to split and knot your thread.

SPLIT STITCH

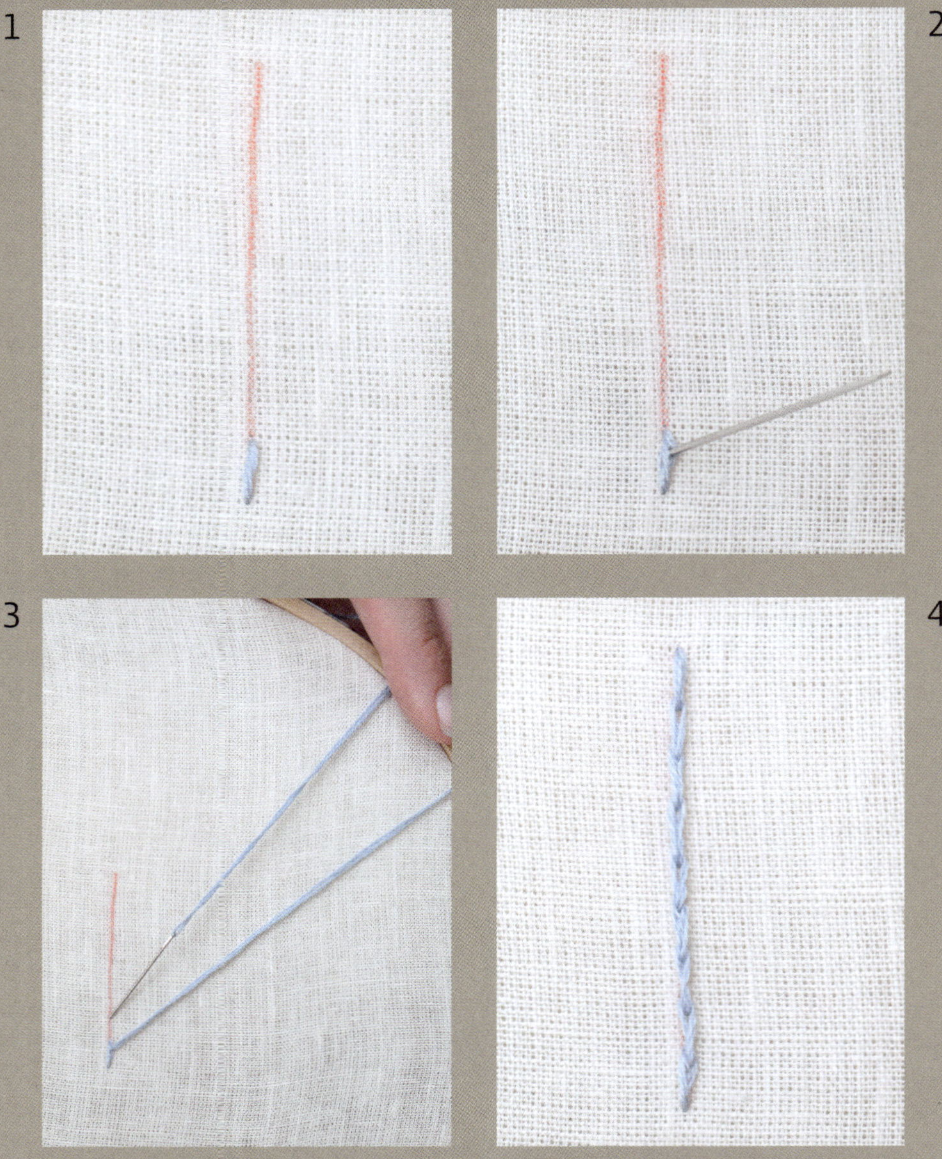

Split stitch is one of the easiest stitches in this book, which is great because it is one of the most frequently used in the projects. I use it to create outlines for shapes and for any line work. I find that the textured line it creates is visually more interesting than a running stitch or backstitch, which is why I use it so often.

DIFFICULTY LEVEL
Easy

1. CREATING THE FIRST STITCH

Working from the back of the fabric, insert the needle at your starting point. Pull the thread all the way through to the front of the fabric. Working from the front, insert your needle back into the fabric approximately one stitch length away (about 4mm [3⁄16in]).

2. SPLIT THE PREVIOUS STITCH

From the back, bring the needle up through the middle of the previous stitch, about two-thirds of the way along – this is why it's called split stitch, because you're splitting the stitch as you come up through it.

3. CONTINUE ALONG THE LINE

From the front, reinsert your needle one stitch length (about 4mm [3⁄16in]) further along the line from where you came up through the previous stitch.

4. REPEAT

Continue this process, repeating the steps until you reach the end of the line. When finished, knot off the thread at the back.

TIP

Since you're using three strands of thread doubled over, there will be six strands in total. When you come up through the previous stitch, try to ensure you have three strands on either side of the needle for a balanced, even look.

SATIN STITCH

Satin stitch is a versatile technique used for filling in solid blocks of colour. It's great for shapes like flower petals and leaves. The technique involves stitching over and under the fabric along the perimeter of your drawn shape to create a smooth, filled area of colour.

DIFFICULTY LEVEL
Easy

1. CREATE THE FIRST STITCH
From the back of the fabric, insert the needle at your starting point. Pull the needle all the way through the fabric until the thread is fully through to the front. From the front, reinsert the needle a stitch width along the perimeter of the outlined shape. Pull the needle through completely, bringing the thread to the back of the fabric.

2. START THE SECOND STITCH
From the back, reinsert the needle next to where you started the previous stitch and pull the needle and thread all the way through to the front.

3. COMPLETE THE SECOND STITCH
From the front, reinsert the needle next to where your previous stitch finished and pull the thread all the way through. You should now have two parallel stitches that are touching.

4. REPEAT
Continue this process until the area has been filled. Once done, knot off at the back.

TIP
For shapes like flower petals, position the stitches at a slight angle for a smoother result. Refer to the photo on page 107 for guidance on how to position stitches to create more natural shapes.

FRENCH KNOT

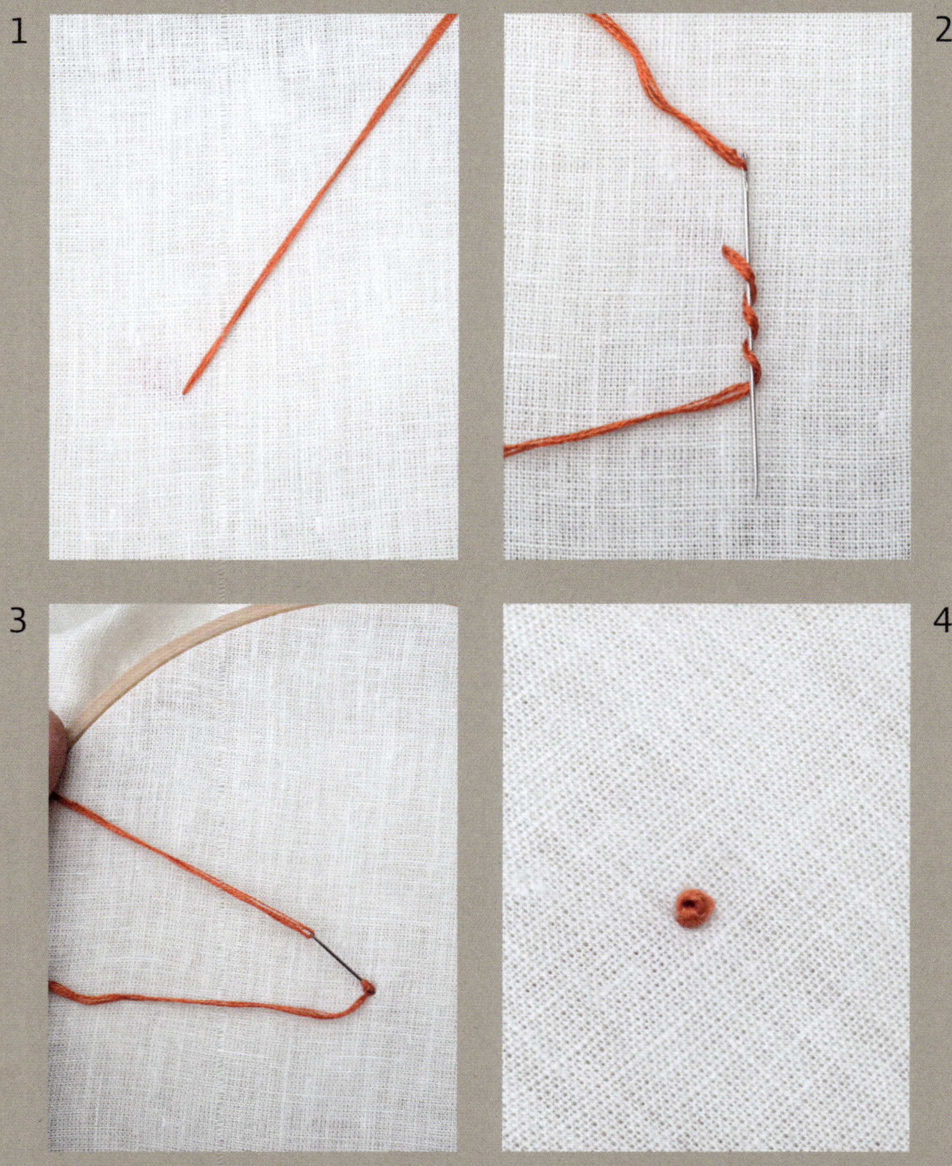

French knots are a brilliant way to create small dots or bobbles. I find they're perfect for adding details like eyes or spots on animals, or for creating texture in flowers. While they can be tricky at first, once you master the technique, they're simple and effective.

DIFFICULTY LEVEL
Medium

1. START AT YOUR DESIRED POINT

From the back of the fabric, insert the needle at the point where you'd like to create your French knot. Pull the needle and the entire length of thread through to the front of the fabric.

2. WRAP THE THREAD

With the needle in one hand, use your other hand to wrap the thread around the needle. I typically wrap it around three times (the number of wraps determines the size of the knot).

3. MAINTAIN TENSION

Keep the thread tightly wound around the needle, and then insert the needle back into the fabric, very close to where it originally came out. Slowly pull the needle through to the back of the fabric, watching as the wraps form a knot on the surface.

4. KNOT OFF THE THREAD

Once you've completed your first French knot, move on to the next one. Don't forget to knot off underneath once you've finished all the French knots or when you've run out of thread.

TIP

When pulling the needle through, take your time and keep an eye on the surface thread to ensure it doesn't get tangled – this can affect the final look of the French knot. Some people find it helps to keep a thumb pressed on the knot while pulling the thread through to avoid tangles.

BLANKET STITCH

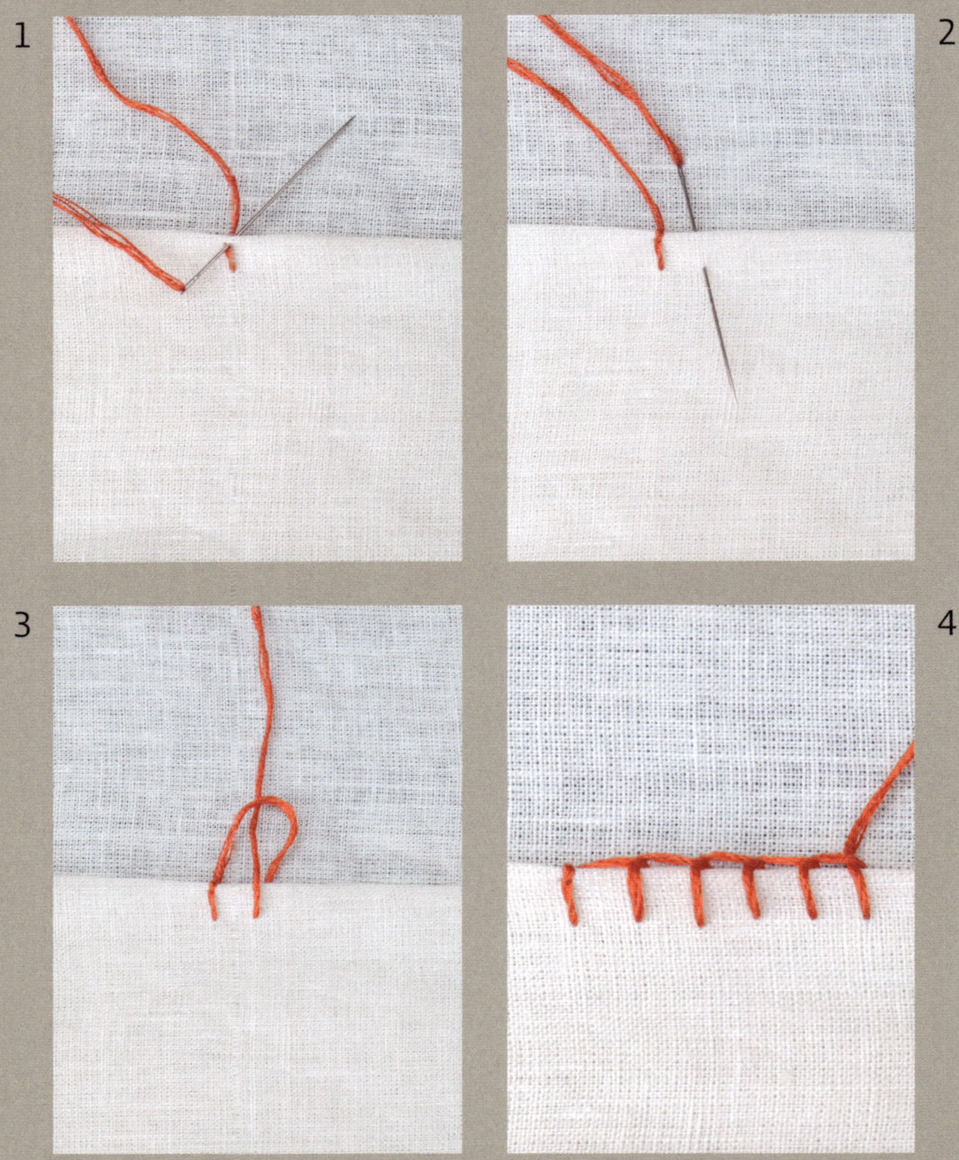

Blanket stitch is a versatile and decorative stitch often used to embellish edges and hems. It's perfect for adding detail along the tops of pockets, necklines and collars. It's relatively easy and less fiddly than the French knot, though it may take a bit of practice. The best part? You don't need a hoop, as this is an edge stitch.

DIFFICULTY LEVEL
Medium

1. CREATING THE FIRST STITCH

Starting from the back of the fabric, begin by inserting the needle about 1cm (⅜in) down from the edge you're working on. Pull the thread all the way through to the front of the fabric. From the front, reinsert the needle close to the fabric edge and then pull it through to the back, creating a stitch that runs vertical to the edge. Next, create a holding stitch for that first stitch – bring the needle around from the back and reinsert it through the same point at the front. This helps to secure your first stitch.

2. START THE BLANKET STITCH

From the back of the fabric, insert the needle about 1cm (⅜in) along from the first stitch.

3. FORM THE LOOP

Pull the needle through the fabric, but before pulling the thread all the way through, insert the needle into the loop created by the thread. Once the needle has passed through the loop, pull the thread tight. You've now created a blanket stitch.

4. REPEAT

Continue this process, spacing the stitches out evenly along the edge. When you reach the end of the edge, tie off the thread securely at the back.

TIPS

- **Spacing:** Keep a consistent distance between the fabric edge and where you position each stitch. Aim for equal spacing between each stitch to achieve a neat, uniform appearance.

- **Tension:** Don't pull the thread too tightly. You want the stitches to lie flat on the surface, and for the fabric to be unpuckered.

WEAVE STITCH

1 2 3 4

Creating a weave stitch is a similar process to darning a hole in a jumper. I love using it in my designs to fill areas like the saddle on a horse or the breast of a bird. It's slightly more challenging than the other stitches, but the beautiful result is well worth the effort. The process involves creating vertical lines that serve as the foundation for weaving through horizontal lines.

DIFFICULTY LEVEL
Medium/hard

1. START CREATING VERTICAL LINES

Working from the back of the fabric, insert the needle at your starting point. Pull the needle and thread all the way through to the front of the fabric. Reinsert the needle at the opposite edge of the shape and pull the thread through to the back, creating a vertical line that runs across the outlined shape. Continue creating vertical lines across the width of the shape. Space the lines about 3mm (⅛in) apart. Start each new vertical stitch line from the same side that the previous stitch finished to avoid long thread lines on the back of the fabric.

2. ADDING A SECOND COLOUR

Taking a second thread colour and repeating step one, create more vertical lines between the first set of vertical lines. You should now have a shape full of vertical lines in two alternating colours.

3. START ADDING HORIZONTAL LINES

Once all the vertical lines are in place, create the horizontal lines using a third thread colour. Insert the needle from the back of the fabric. Using the needle, weave over and under each alternating vertical thread. Once you reach the end of the row, insert the needle and re-emerge approximately 2mm (1⁄16in) below to create a new horizontal line.

4. ALTERNATE WEAVE SEQUENCE

For each new horizontal line, use the opposite weave sequence to the previous row. For example, if your first horizontal line went over and then under the vertical threads, the next one should start under and then go over. Continue this process until the entire area is filled with woven lines.

TIPS

- **Neat rows:** As you weave, use the needle to gently push up the previous rows of weaving to keep them neat and tightly packed together.
- **Colours:** This technique is more technical than the others. All the weave designs in this book use three thread colours: two alternating colours for the vertical lines and one colour for the horizontal lines. If you prefer a simpler approach you can still create beautiful designs using just two colours.

EMBROIDERY

MOTIFS

FISH &

FLORA JACKET

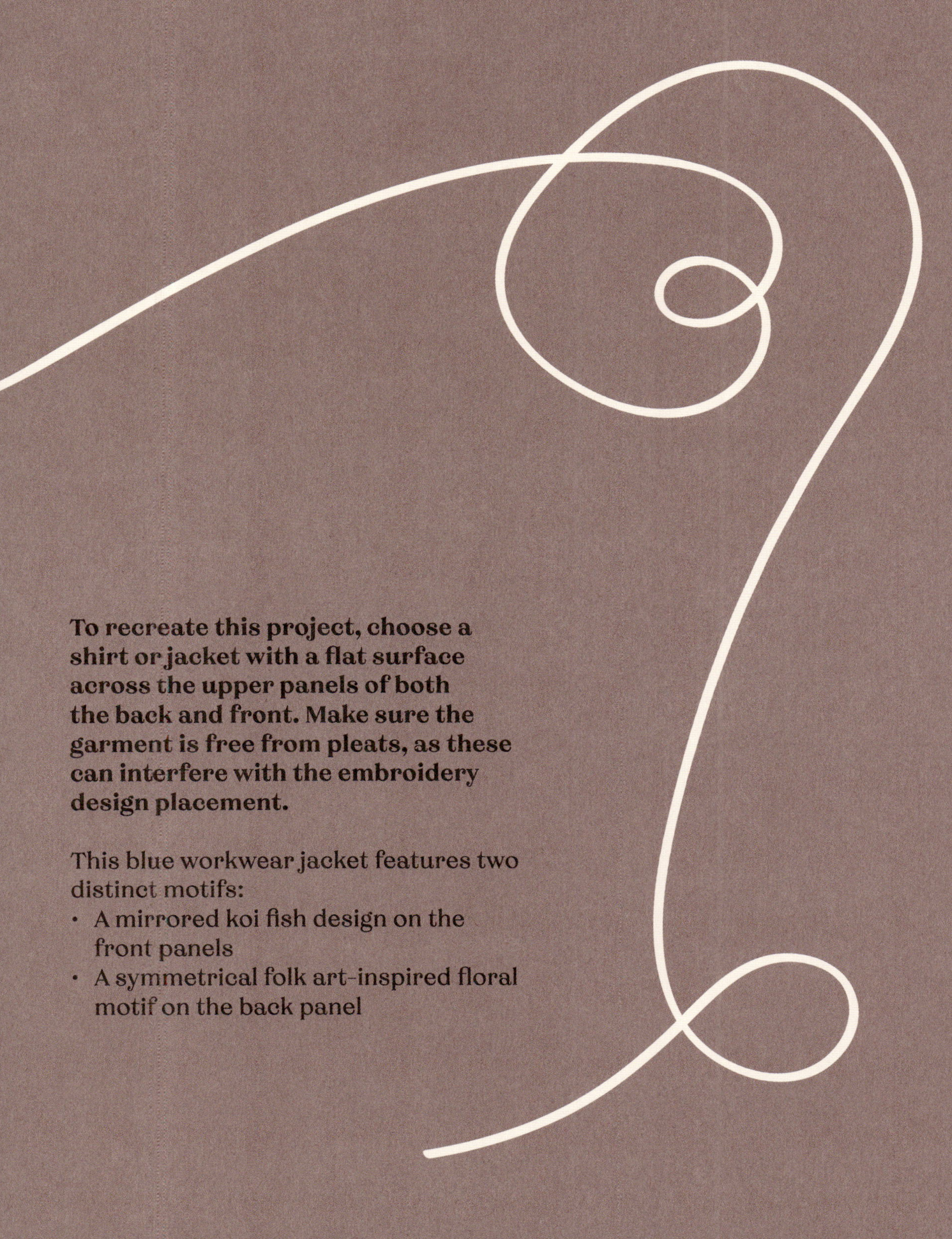

To recreate this project, choose a shirt or jacket with a flat surface across the upper panels of both the back and front. Make sure the garment is free from pleats, as these can interfere with the embroidery design placement.

This blue workwear jacket features two distinct motifs:

- A mirrored koi fish design on the front panels
- A symmetrical folk art-inspired floral motif on the back panel

KOI FISH

This monochromatic design uses only two stitching techniques, making it the ideal project for beginners. You won't need to change thread colours constantly, which simplifies the process. I used an off-white thread but feel free to choose any colour that complements your chosen garment.

LEVEL

Easy

TOOLS

- 1 x scissors
- 1 x embroidery needle
- 1 x embroidery hoop

THREAD

Anchor Stranded Cotton Mouliné embroidery thread in off-white (# 00830)

STITCHES USED IN THIS MOTIF

- Split stitch
- French knots

Template is at 75%. For the correct size, increase the template by 125%.

INSTRUCTIONS

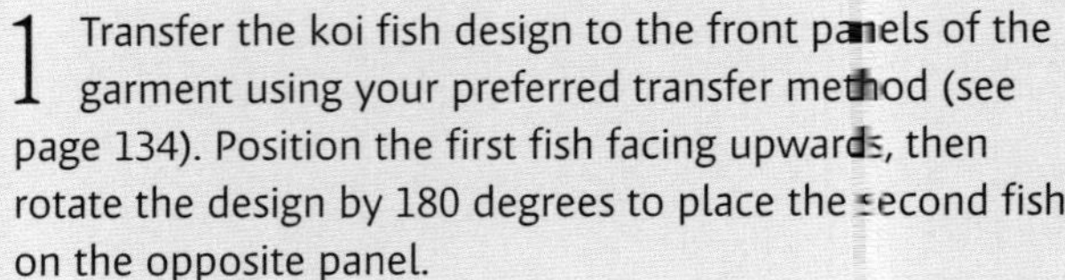

1 Transfer the koi fish design to the front panels of the garment using your preferred transfer method (see page 134). Position the first fish facing upwards, then rotate the design by 180 degrees to place the second fish on the opposite panel.

2 Work split stitch over all the lines for the first fish in the design. Start by outlining the fish, then move on to the details within the fins. Next, stitch along the swirls on the fish's body up to the gills and finish with the lines for the fish's 'whiskers'.

3 Create the fish's eye using a French knot. Make sure you use three wraps for the knot.

4 Repeat steps 2 and 3 for the second fish on the opposite side of the garment.

Template is at 75%. For the correct
size, increase the template by 125%

FLORAL CURLICUE

This design is inspired by a blend of traditional Polish folk art-style flowers and the symmetry of floral patterns seen in Art Nouveau. Like the koi fish design, this motif is also monochromatic. I chose an off-white thread to contrast with the navy-blue garment, but feel free to select any colour that complements your fabric.

LEVEL

Easy

TOOLS

- 1 x scissors
- 1 x embroidery needle
- 1 x embroidery hoop

THREAD

Anchor Stranded Cotton Mouliné embroidery thread in off-white (# 00830)

STITCHES USED IN THIS MOTIF

- Split stitch
- French knots

INSTRUCTIONS

1 Transfer the floral design to the back panel of the garment using your preferred transfer method (see page 134). Position the flower so that it is right in the centre.

2 Work split stitch over all the lines in the design. Since this design is a continuous loop, feel free to start at any point you like.

3 Once all the line work is complete, use French knots to fill in the dots at the centre of the flower. I used three wraps for each knot.

FLOWERS & FLIGHT

TROUSERS

To recreate this project, start by selecting a pair of trousers. Aim for a fit that's slightly loose on the leg, but not so baggy that the design won't sit nicely. You also need to ensure the trousers are wide enough to comfortably accommodate the embroidery hoop and to allow you to work from inside the leg. The techniques shown here can also be applied to a blouse or jacket.

These embroidered trousers feature three distinct motifs:

- A flying bird
- A bird carrying a flower
- A decorative stitch on the back pocket

BIRD IN FLIGHT

This bird-in-flight motif is the perfect size and shape for embroidery on trousers. I recommend positioning it just above the knee, as this area offers a flat, stable surface with minimal drape, ensuring the design stands out beautifully.

LEVEL

Medium

TOOLS

- 1 x scissors
- 1 x embroidery needle
- 1 x embroidery hoop

THREAD

DMC Stranded Cotton in yellow (# 3046)
Anchor Stranded Cotton Mouliné embroidery thread in the following shades:

- Plum (# 00897)
- Blue (# 00939)
- Dark orange (# 00326)
- Mauve (# 00896)

STITCHES USED IN THIS MOTIF

- Split stitch
- French knots
- Satin stitch
- Weave stitch

Template is at 75%. For the correct size, increase the template by 125%.

INSTRUCTIONS

1 Transfer the bird design to your chosen garment using your preferred transfer method (see page 134).

2 Using the plum thread (Anchor # 00897), work split stitch around the outline of the bird.

3 Continuing with split stitch, create the lines on the bird's tail and wings, as well as the three swirls on the bird's head. Use blue (Anchor # 00939) for these details.

4 While you are still using the blue thread, create the bird's eye with a French knot. Wrap the thread three times to complete the knot.

5 Create the dots on the bird's wings by working French knots, each with three wraps. Use dark orange (Anchor # 00326) for these.

6 For the dots on the tail, work French knots, alternating between two colours: mauve (Anchor # 00896) and yellow (DMC # 3046). Work each knot with three wraps.

7 Use dark orange (# 00326) to fill in the bird's beak with satin stitch. Start at the tip and use slanted stitches to create a smooth finish.

8 To fill the bird's chest, use a weave stitch. Start by creating vertical lines, alternating between blue (Anchor # 00939) and mauve (Anchor # 00896). Once the vertical lines are complete, weave horizontal lines using yellow (DMC # 3046) to complete the basketweave effect.

Template is at 75%. For the correct size, increase the template by 125%.

BIRD CARRYING A FLOWER

This motif of a bird carrying a flower is perfect for trousers, as it works well with a longer area of fabric. Placing the bird slightly lower on the leg, as opposed to the flying bird motif, allows for an interesting interaction between the two. It creates the illusion that they are soaring toward each other, adding dynamic movement to the design.

LEVEL

Medium

TOOLS

- 1 x scissors
- 1 x embroidery needle
- 1 x embroidery hoop

THREAD

DMC Stranded Cotton in yellow (# 3046)
Anchor Stranded Cotton Mouliné embroidery thread in the following shades:

- Plum (# 00897)
- Dark orange (# 00326)
- Mauve (# 00896)
- Blue (# 00939)

STITCHES USED IN THIS MOTIF

- Split stitch
- French knots
- Satin stitch
- Weave stitch

INSTRUCTIONS

1 Transfer the bird and flower design to your chosen garment using your preferred transfer method (see page 134).

2 Using the plum thread (Anchor # 00897), outline the bird's shape with split stitch.

3 Work over the lines on the bird's tail and wings with split stitch. Use dark orange thread (Anchor # 00326) for these parts.

4 Create the dots on the bird's wings with French knots in yellow (DMC # 3046) thread. Each French knot is made with three wraps.

5 Create the dots on the bird's wings with French knots in mauve (Anchor # 00896) thread. Each French knot is made with three wraps.

6 Use a weave stitch to fill in the bird's chest. Start by creating vertical lines, alternating between dark orange (Anchor # 00326) and blue (Anchor # 00939). Once the vertical lines are complete, weave horizontal lines using mauve (Anchor # 00896) to finish the basketweave effect.

7 Using split stitch, create the flower stem in blue (Anchor # 00939). Leave a small gap in the stitching where the bird's beak will overlap.

8 Still using blue (Anchor # 00939), work satin stitch to fill in the leaves.

9 Use split stitch to outline the flower with dark orange (Anchor # 00326).

10 Use satin stitch to fill in the middle of the petals. I chose mauve (Anchor # 00896) for these.

11 Using yellow (DMC # 3046) thread, work French knots to add the dot details in the flower centre.

12 Now that the flower is complete, fill in the bird's beak with satin stitch using yellow (DMC # 3046 thread.

13 Use split stitch and yellow (DMC # 3046) thread to work over the swirls on the bird's head.

14 For the finishing touch, create the bird's eye by working a French knot, wrapping the thread three times. I used blue (Anchor # 00939) for the eye.

POCKET EMBELLISHMENT

This is a quick and easy motif that doesn't require a hoop, perfect for adding some embellishment to any pocket flap.

LEVEL

Easy

TOOLS

- 1 x scissors
- 1 x embroidery needle

THREAD

Anchor Stranded Cotton Mouliné embroidery thread in the following shades:

- Dark orange (# 00326)
- Mauve (# 00896)

STITCHES USED IN THIS MOTIF

- Blanket stitch
- French knots

INSTRUCTIONS

1 You can either mark out the spacing for the design as a guide or work freehand for this embellishment if you prefer a more organic feel.

2 Using dark orange (Anchor # 00326) thread, work blanket stitch along the edge of the pocket flap, starting from one corner.

3 Once the blanket stitch is complete, use French knots to add little mauve (Anchor # 00896) dots between the blanket stitches. Each knot should have three wraps.

TIGER & BIRD TOP

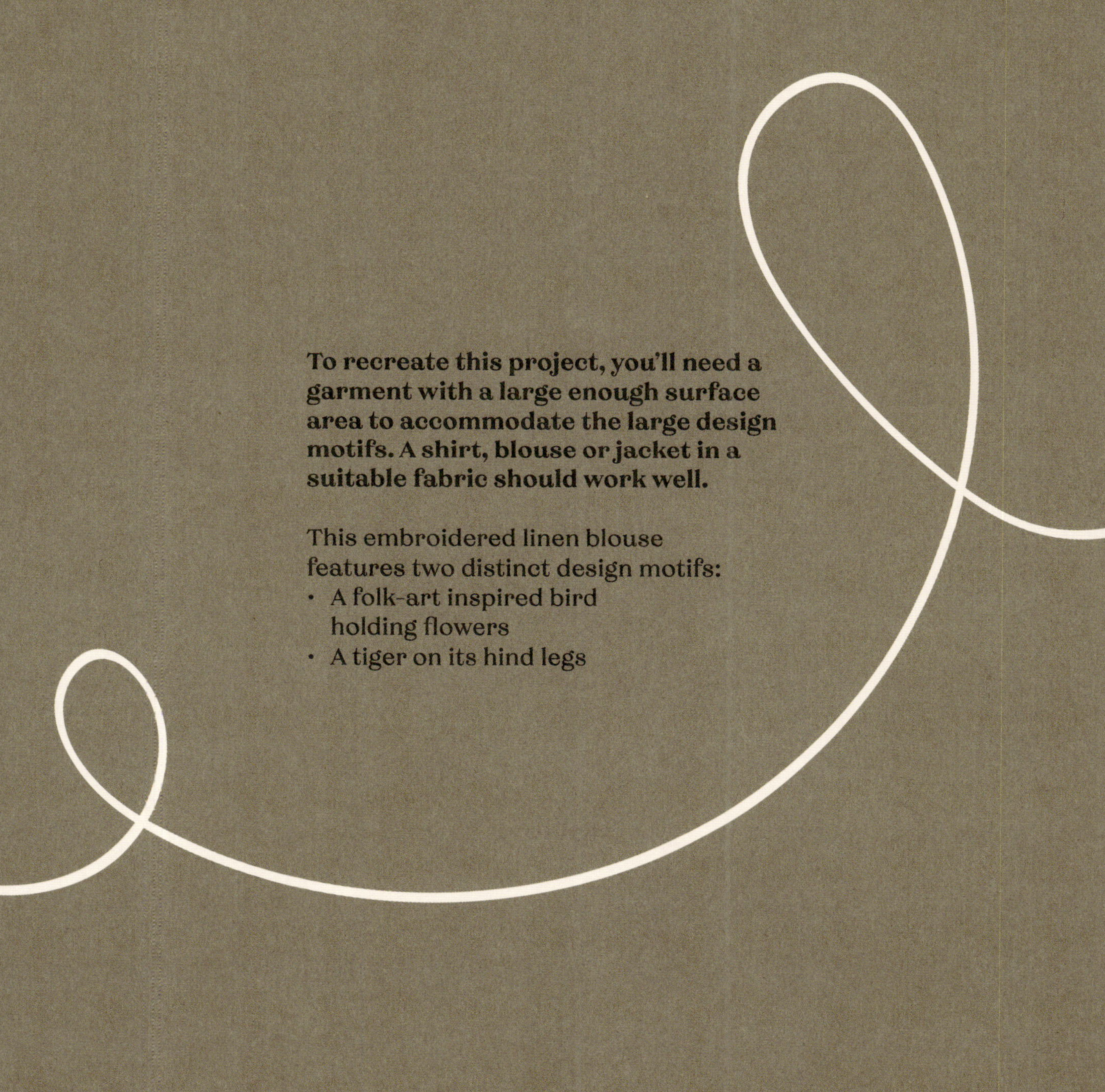

To recreate this project, you'll need a garment with a large enough surface area to accommodate the large design motifs. A shirt, blouse or jacket in a suitable fabric should work well.

This embroidered linen blouse features two distinct design motifs:

- A folk-art inspired bird holding flowers
- A tiger on its hind legs

Template is at 50%. Fo
the correct size, increa
the template by 150%.

BIRD HOLDING FLOWERS

This large, folk-art inspired motif depicts a bird carrying two flowers. This is a great project if you want to embroider a substantial area of a garment.

LEVEL

Medium/hard

TOOLS

- 1 x scissors
- 1 x embroidery needle
- 1 x embroidery hoop

THREAD

Anchor Stranded Cotton Mouliné embroidery thread in the following shades:

- Red (# 00341)
- Tomato red (# 01015)
- Plum (# 00897)
- Pink (# 01027)
- Rusty orange (# 00309)

STITCHES USED IN THIS MOTIF

- Split stitch
- Satin stitch
- French knots
- Weave stitch

INSTRUCTIONS

1 Begin by transferring the image to the garment using your preferred transfer method (see page 134).

2 Using split stitch, outline the stems of both flowers. I used red (Anchor # 00341) for this step.

3 Using tomato red (Anchor # 01015), work satin stitch to fill in all the leaves on the stems.

4 Work satin stitch to fill in the petals of the flowers. Use plum thread (Anchor # 00897) for this.

5 Add French knots to create the bobbles in the centres of the flowers using pink (Anchor # 01027). Wrap the thread around the needle three times for the French knots.

6 Now that the flowers are complete, move on to the bird. Start by outlining the bird's body using split stitch. I used plum thread (Anchor # 00897) for this. For the bird's eye, work a French knot in the same colour.

7 Fill in the bird's beak and legs in satin stitch with pink (Anchor # 01027) thread.

8 Use split stitch to outline the feathers on the bird's head and the lines within the tail and wing. Use rusty orange (Anchor # 00309) for the head feathers and pink (Anchor # 01027) for the wing and tail.

9 Using tomato red (Anchor # 01015), work French knots to create the dots on the bird's wing and tail.

10 The bird's breast is filled with weave stitch. Start by creating vertical lines, alternating between two colours – tomato red (Anchor # 01015) and rusty orange (Anchor # 00309). Once the vertical lines are complete, weave in the horizontal lines using pink (Anchor # 01027).

TIGER ON ITS HIND LEGS

This tiger motif is a great choice for covering a large area. Despite its size, it's relatively simple, requiring minimal detail. I don't often repeat motifs when creating my designs, but this is one I find myself returning to time and time again.

LEVEL

Easy

TOOLS

- 1 x scissors
- 1 x embroidery needle
- 1 x embroidery hoop

THREAD

Anchor Stranded Cotton Mouliné embroidery thread in the following shades:

- Plum (# 00897)
- Rusty orange (# 00309)
- Red (# 00341)
- Pink (# 01027)

STITCHES USED IN THIS MOTIF

- Split stitch
- Satin stitch
- French knots

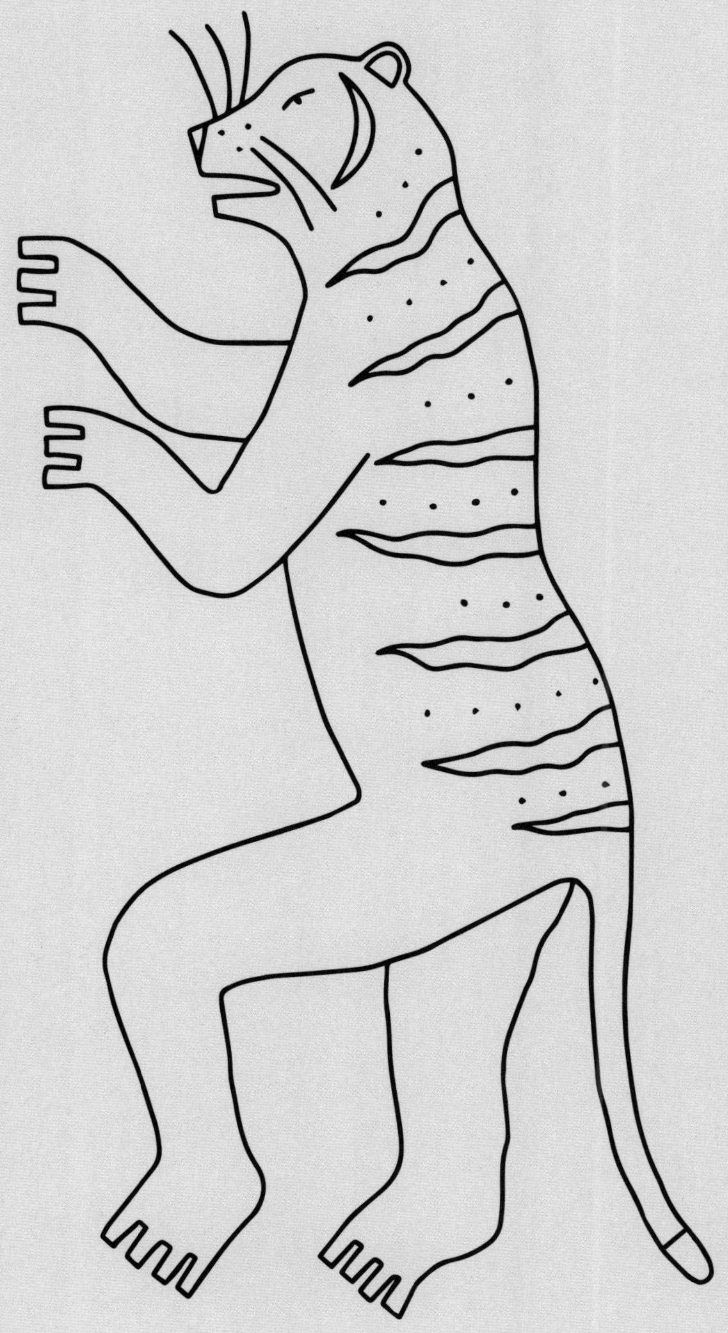

Template is at 50%. For the correct size, increase the template by 150%.

INSTRUCTIONS

1 Begin by transferring the design to the garment using your preferred transfer method (see page 134).

2 Use split stitch to outline the tiger's shape. For this, I used plum thread (Anchor # 00897).

3 Continuing with plum thread (Anchor # 00897), work three French knots to create the dots near the tiger's whiskers and work one more French knot for the eye. Use split stitch to outline the eyelid.

4 Use split stitch for the tiger's whiskers and satin stitch for the nose and the centre of the ear. Work these details in rusty orange (Anchor # 00309).

5 Use red (Anchor # 00341) thread to work satin stitch to fill in the tiger's stripes.

6 To create the spots between the tiger's stripes, work three-wrap French knots using pink thread (Anchor # 01027).

7 For the final touch, use satin stitch to fill in the end of the tiger's tail. Use rusty orange (Anchor # 00309) to do this.

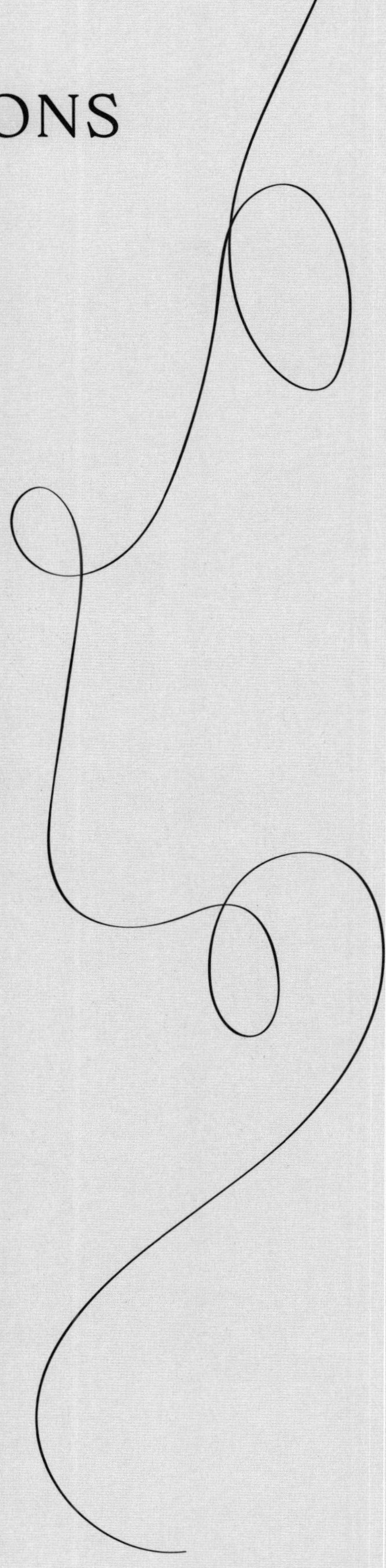

FLOWERS

To recreate this project, choose a garment with a visible button placket running down the centre front for the decorative stitching. If your garment doesn't have this feature, it's still possible to embroider the other two motifs as they can be applied to any garment with a large enough flat surface, free of darts or pleats.

This embroidered blouse features three distinct motifs:

- Folk-art inspired floral motif
- Decorative stitching along the button placket
- A fawn carrying a tulip

& FAWN BLOUSE

MIRRORED FLOWER MOTIF

This simple, yet playful folk-art inspired floral motif is perfect for embellishing the shoulder area of a garment.

LEVEL

Easy

TOOLS

- 1 x scissors
- 1 x embroidery needle
- 1 x embroidery hoop

THREAD

Anchor Stranded Cotton Mouliné embroidery thread in the following shades:

- Orangey red (# 00340)
- Light blue (# 00939)
- Light teal (# 00876)

STITCHES USED IN THIS MOTIF

- Split stitch
- Satin stitch

Template is at 100%

INSTRUCTIONS

1 Transfer the floral motif to the garment using your preferred transfer method (see page 134). Mirror the design on both shoulders for a balanced look.

2 Using orangey red (Anchor # 00340) thread, outline the flowers with split stitch.

3 Fill in the areas inside the flowers with a slanted satin stitch. Use light blue (Anchor # 00939) for this part.

4 Use split stitch to outline the stems and leaves of the plants. I used light teal (Anchor # 00876) for the stems and leaves.

DECORATIVE STITCHING ON PLACKET

This project is a fun way to add a decorative touch to the button placket of any shirt or jacket. I recommend freehand drawing your design, as each garment's button placket will vary in size. Drawing your own design means you can customize it to best suit the distance between the buttons.

Using a hoop isn't super easy for this project, due to the proximity of the design to the edge of the fabric. I suggest working without a hoop; just be careful not to create too much tension in the stitches to prevent the fabric from bunching.

LEVEL

Easy

TOOLS

- 1 x scissors
- 1 x embroidery needle

THREAD

Anchor Stranded Cotton Mouliné embroidery thread in the following shades:

- Dark blue (# 00922)
- Orangey red (# 00340)

STITCHES USED IN THIS MOTIF

- Split stitch
- French knots

INSTRUCTIONS

1 Using a transfer pen, mark out the squiggly lines along the button placket. You can add as many curves as you like, but I recommend keeping a consistent number between each button for a balanced look. I drew three curves per line.

2 Using dark blue (Anchor # 00922) thread, work split stitch over the curved lines. Most button plackets have a double layer of fabric (like a hem), so for a neat finish, you can insert the needle between the two layers of fabric and then re-emerge to start the next stitch. This will hide the thread between the layers. If this feels too tricky, or if you don't have a double layer of fabric, you can knot off the thread and restart between each section to avoid thread spanning the back of the buttonhole.

3 Use French knots to create decorative bobbles between the curves on the lines you've just stitched. You can apply the same technique described in step 2 to hide the thread between the fabric layers. I used orangey red (Anchor # 00340) for the French knots.

Template is at 75%. For the correct size, increase the template by 125%.

FAWN WITH A TULIP

This folk-art inspired fawn motif is the most intricate project in the book, involving a variety of colours and stitches.

LEVEL
Medium/hard

TOOLS
- 1 x scissors
- 1 x embroidery needle
- 1 x embroidery hoop

THREAD
Anchor Stranded Cotton Mouliné embroidery thread in the following shades:
- Yellow (# 00279)
- Chartreuse (# 00280)
- Mauve (# 00896)
- Orangey red (# 00340)
- Dark blue (# 00922)
- Light teal (# 00876)
- Brown (# 01050)

STITCHES USED IN THIS MOTIF
- Split stitch
- Satin stitch
- French knots
- Weave stitch

INSTRUCTIONS

1 Begin by transferring the motif to the garment using your preferred transfer method (see page 134).

2 Use yellow (Anchor # 00279) thread to work split stitch around the outline of the flower stem. With the same colour, fill in the plant's leaves using satin stitch.

3 To add detail to the plant stem, I used a subtly different shade of thread, chartreuse (Anchor # 00280). Use chartreuse to place French knots over the split-stitched stem. Then, use split stitch and chartreuse to create lines along the leaves, working over the satin stitch from step 2.

4 Use slanted satin stitch to fill in the flower petals. I used mauve (Anchor # 896) for the outer petals and orangey red (Anchor # 00340) for the centre petal.

5 Work three French knots at the base of the flower using dark blue (Anchor # 00922).

6 Now that the flower is complete, move on to the fawn. Begin by using split stitch to outline the fawn's body with dark blue (Anchor # 00922).

7 Use satin stitch to fill in the nose and tail areas, using light teal (Anchor # 00876). Add a French knot at the end of the tail using three wraps of the same colour.

8 Fill in the hooves with satin stitch using yellow (Anchor # 00279).

9 Use weave stitch to fill the fawn's saddle. Start by creating vertical lines in two alternating colours – brown (Anchor # 01050) and light teal (Anchor # 00876). Once the vertical lines are complete, weave in the horizontal lines using a third colour, yellow (Anchor # 00279).

10 Outline the weave area with split stitch using mauve (Anchor # 896). Then, using orangey red (Anchor # 00340), add a second split stitch line along the outer edge.

11 Once all the line work is done, embellish the design with French knots. I used brown (Anchor # 01050) for the eye, for dots on the body and within the saddle decoration. I also used light teal (Anchor # 00876) for the dots along the outline of the saddle.

SEAHORSE,

To recreate this project, you'll need a garment with a large enough surface area to accommodate the seahorse because it is a large motif. A shirt, blouse or jacket in a suitable fabric should work.

This embroidered linen shirt features three distinct motifs:

- A large seahorse
- A clamshell
- Two little fish

SHELL & FISH SHIRT

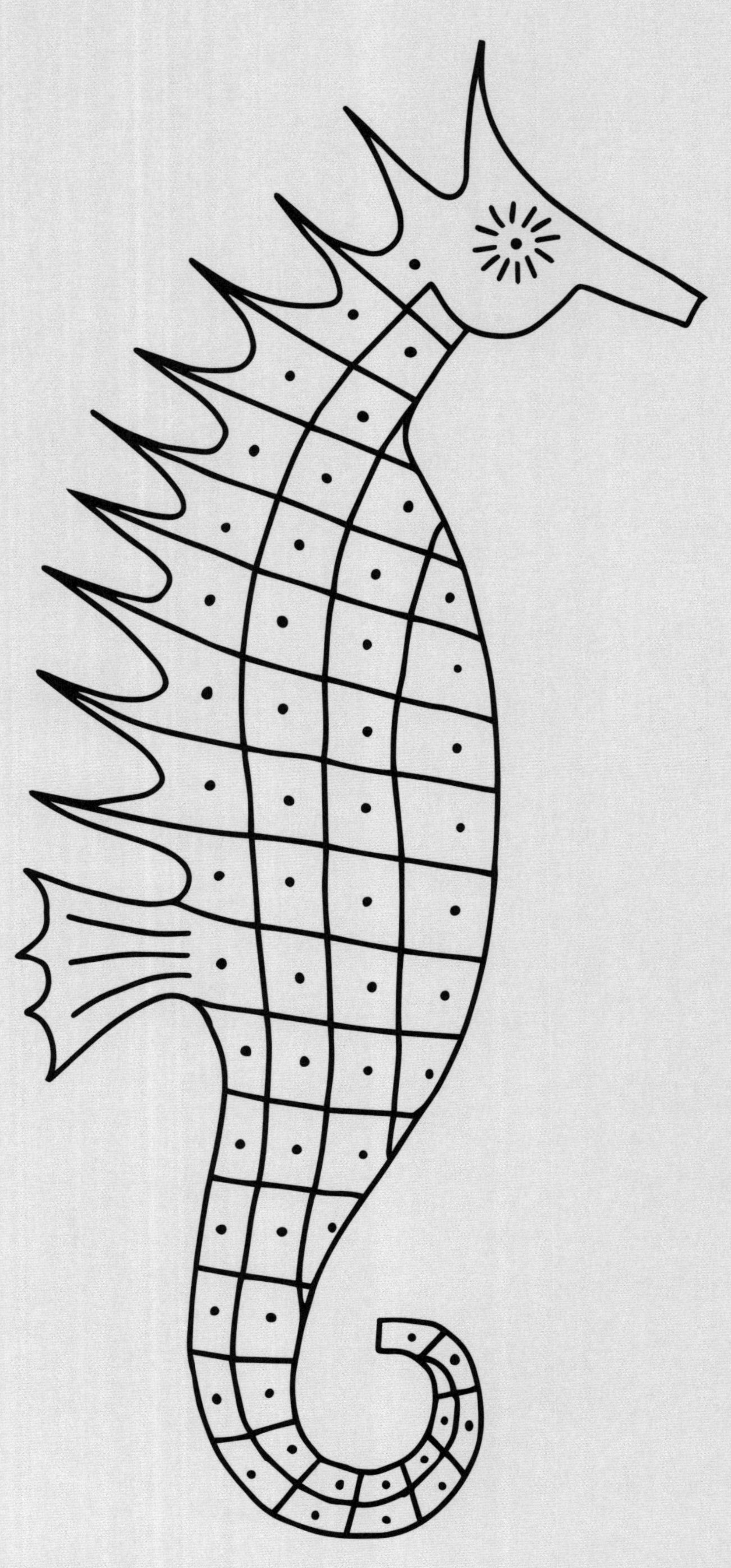

Template is at 75%. For the correct size, increase the template by 125%.

SEAHORSE

This large seahorse motif involves just two stitching techniques and is a fantastic choice if you're looking for a project that covers a substantial area.

LEVEL

Easy

TOOLS

- 1 x scissors
- 1 x embroidery needle
- 1 x embroidery hoop

THREAD

Anchor Stranded Cotton Mouliné embroidery thread in the following shades:

- Soft orange (# 00884)
- Slate blue (# 00922)
- Green blue (# 00850)
- Mossy green (# 00281)
- Indigo (# 00122)
- Pale pink (# 01017)

STITCHES USED IN THIS MOTIF

- Split stitch
- French knots

INSTRUCTIONS

1 Transfer the design to the garment using your preferred transfer method (see page 134).

2 First, outline the body of the seahorse using split stitch. I alternated between two colours to do this. You can use just one colour if you prefer, but if you'd like to use two, I recommend stitching one colour first, leaving gaps where you want the second colour, and then coming back to complete the outline with the second colour. I used soft orange (Anchor # 00884) and slate blue (Anchor # 00922).

3 Using split stitch once more, work over the horizontal lines running across the seahorse's body. Alternate between two colours: green blue (Anchor # 00850) and mossy green (Anchor # 00281).

4 Use mossy green (Anchor # 00281) to create the three lines on the seahorse's fin with split stitch.

5 Now that all the horizontal lines are complete, move on to the vertical lines. Use indigo (Anchor # 00122) for these split stitch lines.

6 The vertical and horizontal lines should have formed a grid-like pattern. Alternating between two colours – pale pink (Anchor # 01017) and soft orange (Anchor # 00884) – add a French knot to each square of the grid.

7 Work a French knot in slate blue (Anchor # 00922) for the seahorse's eye. Wrap the thread three times around the needle when making the French knot.

8 To finish the design, add some individual stitches around the seahorse's eye area. I used mossy green (Anchor # 00281) for this.

CLAMSHELL

This clamshell motif is simple and relatively quick to work. It's particularly effective for the breast pocket of a shirt.

LEVEL

Easy

TOOLS

- 1 x scissors
- 1 x embroidery needle
- 1 x embroidery hoop

THREAD

Anchor Stranded Cotton Mouliné embroidery thread in the following shades:

- Slate blue (# 00922)
- Green blue (# 00850)
- Soft orange (# 00884)
- Pale pink (# 01017)

STITCHES USED IN THIS MOTIF

- Split stitch
- French knots
- Satin stitch

Template is at 50%. For the correct size, increase the template by 150%.

INSTRUCTIONS

1 Transfer the design to the garment using your preferred transfer method (see page 134).

2 Work split stitch around the perimeter of the shell to form the outline. I used slate blue (Anchor # 00922) for this.

3 Use green blue (Anchor # 00850) thread and split stitch to form the lines within the shell.

4 Add columns of dots between the lines in the shell by working French knots in soft orange (Anchor # 00884). Wrap the thread three times for each French knot.

5 Fill in the circular pearl in the centre of the shell with satin stitch using pale pink (Anchor # 01017) thread.

6 For the finishing touches, use split stitch to add little swirls in the bottom corners of the shell. You can use soft orange (Anchor # 00884) or another colour of your choice for this detail.

Template is at 10(

TWO SMALL FISH

This motif, featuring two small fish, is a great small-scale design that can be placed in a variety of areas on a garment.

LEVEL

Easy

TOOLS

- 1 x scissors
- 1 x embroidery needle
- 1 x embroidery hoop

THREAD

Anchor Stranded Cotton Mouliné embroidery thread in the following shades:

- Mossy green (# 00281)
- Soft orange (# 00884)
- Slate blue (# 00922)
- Indigo (# 00122)
- Green blue (# 00850)

STITCHES USED IN THIS MOTIF

- Split stitch
- French knots
- Satin stitch

INSTRUCTIONS

1 Transfer the design to the garment using your preferred transfer method (see page 134).

2 Work split stitch around the outline of the body of each fish. I used mossy green (Anchor # 00281) for this.

3 Use soft orange (Anchor # 00884) to work satin stitch to fill in the fish's fins along the sides of their bodies.

4 Using split stitch and slate blue (Anchor # 00922), work over the line separating the fish's heads from their bodies. Then, with the same colour, create a French knot for each fish's eye. Wrap the thread three times for each French knot.

5 Create the chevron lines running along the body of each fish and the line separating the tail from the body with split stitch. Use indigo (# 00122) thread for these lines.

6 To finish off the design, add French knots to create the spots along the fish's bodies. I alternated between two colours to do this: green blue (Anchor # 00850) and soft orange (Anchor # 00884), using one colour per section.

THREE
FISH

WRAP
TOP

I used an asymmetrical wrap top for this project to show how it's possible to work with a garment's shape to create interesting compositions. However, the motifs could be used on any garment in a suitable fabric and rearranged to suit the area you're working with. The flower motif is great for a shoulder area, but the fish could be used on their own or together to create varied arrangements.

This embroidered linen wrap top features two distinct motifs:

- A floral shoulder design
- A woven fish (repeated)

SHOULDER FLOWER

Creating this motif is a great opportunity to perfect your slanted satin stitch, as it features plenty of organic, curved shapes in the leaves and petals.

LEVEL

Easy

TOOLS

- 1 x scissors
- 1 x embroidery needle
- 1 x embroidery hoop

THREAD

Anchor Stranded Cotton Mouliné embroidery thread in the following shades:

- Chartreuse (# 00280)
- Plum (# 00897)
- Red (# 00341)
- Mauve (# 00896)

STITCHES USED IN THIS MOTIF

- Split stitch
- Satin stitch

Template is at 100%

INSTRUCTIONS

1 Transfer the flower and fish designs to the garment using your preferred transfer method (see page 134).

2 Using split stitch, work your way along the flower stem. To give the stem some thickness, create two parallel lines of split stitch that touch. I used chartreuse (# 00280) for this.

3 Fill in the leaves with slanted satin stitch in chartreuse (# 00280).

4 Use slanted satin stitch for the petals and alternate between three colours to add depth to the flower. I used plum (# 00897), red (# 00341) and mauve (# 00896)

WOVEN FISH

This intricate fish motif is small but packed with techniques. The instructions opposite describe how to stitch one fish, but you can repeat the steps as many times as needed to create a design with multiple fish.

LEVEL

Medium/hard

TOOLS

- 1 x scissors
- 1 x embroidery needle
- 1 x embroidery hoop

THREAD

Anchor Stranded Cotton Mouliné embroidery thread in the following shades:

- Light teal (# 00876)
- Plum (# 00897)
- Ochre (# 00309)
- Sky blue (# 00121)
- Red (# 00341)
- Chartreuse (# 00281)
- Slate blue (# 00922)

STITCHES USED IN THIS MOTIF

- Split stitch
- Satin stitch
- French knots
- Weave stitch

Template is at 100%

INSTRUCTIONS

1 Using light teal (# 00876) thread, outline the body of the fish with split stitch. Complete the lines that separate the fish's head from its body and the tail from the body using the same colour and stitch.

2 Fill the middle section of the fish's body with weave stitch. This will be intricate and time-consuming, but the result is worth it. Start by creating vertical lines, alternating between two colours – plum (# 00897) and ochre (# 00309). Once the vertical lines are in place, begin weaving in the horizontal lines using sky blue (# 00121).

3 Work the fish's fins in satin stitch using red (# 00341) thread.

4 Still using red (# 00341), go over the lines within the fish's tail with split stitch.

5 Create French knots to form the spots on the fish's tail. Each knot should have three wraps. I alternated between two colours, chartreuse (# 00281) and sky blue (# 00121), for this.

6 Work another three-wrap French knot to form the fish's eye using slate blue (# 00922) thread.

7 For the final step, make small, individual stitches to fill in the area surrounding the eye using chartreuse (# 00281).

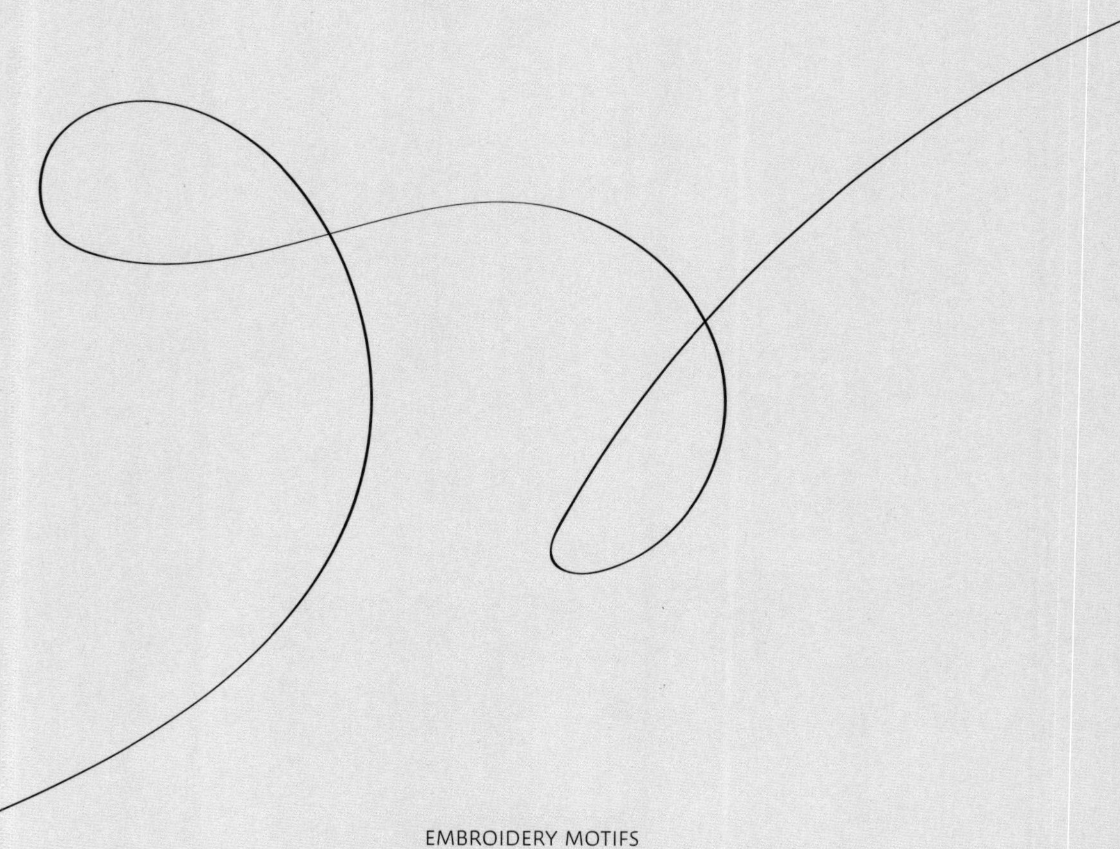

PARROT & POPPY JACKET

The beautiful motifs in this project are quite large-scale, which makes for a really impactful design. It does mean you'll need to embroider them on a garment with a large surface area. A shirt, blouse or jacket in a suitable fabric would be best.

This embroidered linen jacket features two distinct design motifs:

- A large poppy
- A parrot on a plant stem
- For the decorative pocket stitching refer to the instructions on page 61.

Temp.ate is at 50%. Fo
the correct size, increa
the template by 150%

POPPY

This large poppy motif has a playful, organic shape and is an excellent choice if you're looking for a project that covers a substantial area.

LEVEL

Easy

TOOLS

- 1 x scissors
- 1 x embroidery needle
- 1 x embroidery hoop

THREAD

DMC Stranded Cotton Embroidery thread in the following shades:

- Pale green (# 0523)
- Cornflower blue (# 0161)
- Sky blue (# 0794)

STITCHES USED IN THIS MOTIF

- Split stitch
- Satin stitch
- French knots

INSTRUCTIONS

1 Begin by transferring the image to the garment using your preferred transfer method (see page 134).

2 Using pale green (# 0523), outline the poppy leaves with split stitch. Then, using the same colour, use split stitch to outline the flower stem. For a thicker stem, work two parallel rows of split stitch that touch each other.

3 Create the lines through the centres of the leaves using split stitch. Use cornflower blue (# 0161) for this detail.

4 Outline the perimeters of the flower petals in split stitch using sky blue (# 0794) thread.

5 Use satin stitch to fill in the inner areas of the flower petals. For the five upper petals I used cornflower blue (# 0161) and for the two lower petals beneath the flower, I used sky blue (# 0794).

6 Create a French knot in the centre of the flower, then fill the empty space within the petals with lots of French knots. Use pale green (# 0523) for these.

PARROT ON A PLANT STEM

This parrot motif is a great option for covering a large surface area with embroidery. It may look like a complex design but it's actually quite easy to embroider, as it's worked primarily in split stitch.

LEVEL

Easy

TOOLS

- 1 x scissors
- 1 x embroidery needle
- 1 x embroidery hoop

THREAD

DMC Stranded Cotton Embroidery thread in the following shades:

- Cornflower blue (# 0161)
- Pale green (# 0523)
- Sky blue (# 0794)

STITCHES USED IN THIS MOTIF

- Split stitch
- Satin stitch
- French knots

Template is at 50%. For the correct size, increase the template by 150%.

INSTRUCTIONS

1 Transfer the design to the garment using your preferred transfer method (see page 134).

2 Using pale green (# 0523) thread, outline the plant's leaves with split stitch. Then, with the same colour, use split stitch to outline the stem. To create a thicker stem, work two parallel rows of split stitch, so that they touch.

3 Use split stitch to create the lines through the centres of the leaves. I used cornflower blue (# 0161) for this detail.

4 Outline all the lines on the parrot's head and body with split stitch. Use pale green (# 0523) for the head, the lines within the wings and the upper part of the parrot's leg. Use sky blue (# 0794) for the outline of the wings and cornflower blue (# 0161) for the tail feathers and the curly feathers on top of the bird's head.

5 Fill in the parrot's beak and feet using satin stitch. Use sky blue (# 0794) for the beak and then cornflower blue (# 0161) for the bird's feet.

6 Create small, individual stitches to add texture to the areas within the bird's head and upper leg. I used pale green (# 0523) for this effect.

7 To finish, work a French knot for the bird's eye and add three-wrap French knots to the area where the head meets the neck. Use cornflower blue (# 0161) for these French knots.

HORSE & BLOOMS

To recreate this project, you'll need a garment with front-facing pockets. I have used a waistcoat, but you can choose any shirt, blouse or jacket that has a front pocket.

This embroidered linen waistcoat features three distinct motifs:

- Pocket blooms
- A horse design (repeated)
- A folk-art style plant

WAISTCOAT

POCKET BLOOMS

This motif provides a wonderful way to add delicate details to front-facing pockets. Adjust the length of the stems to fit the shape of the garment you're working on. In the example here, I added two pocket flowers to a waistcoat – both are slight variations of the same design. By changing the leaf placement, stem length and flower shape, you can easily add variety.

LEVEL

Easy

TOOLS

- 1 x scissors
- 1 x embroidery needle
- 1 x embroidery hoop

THREAD

Anchor Stranded Cotton Mouliné embroidery thread in the following shades:

- Green blue (# 00850)
- Light blue (# 00939)
- Orange (# 01004)
- Pale pink (# 01017)

STITCHES USED IN THIS MOTIF

- Split stitch
- Satin stitch
- Blanket stitch

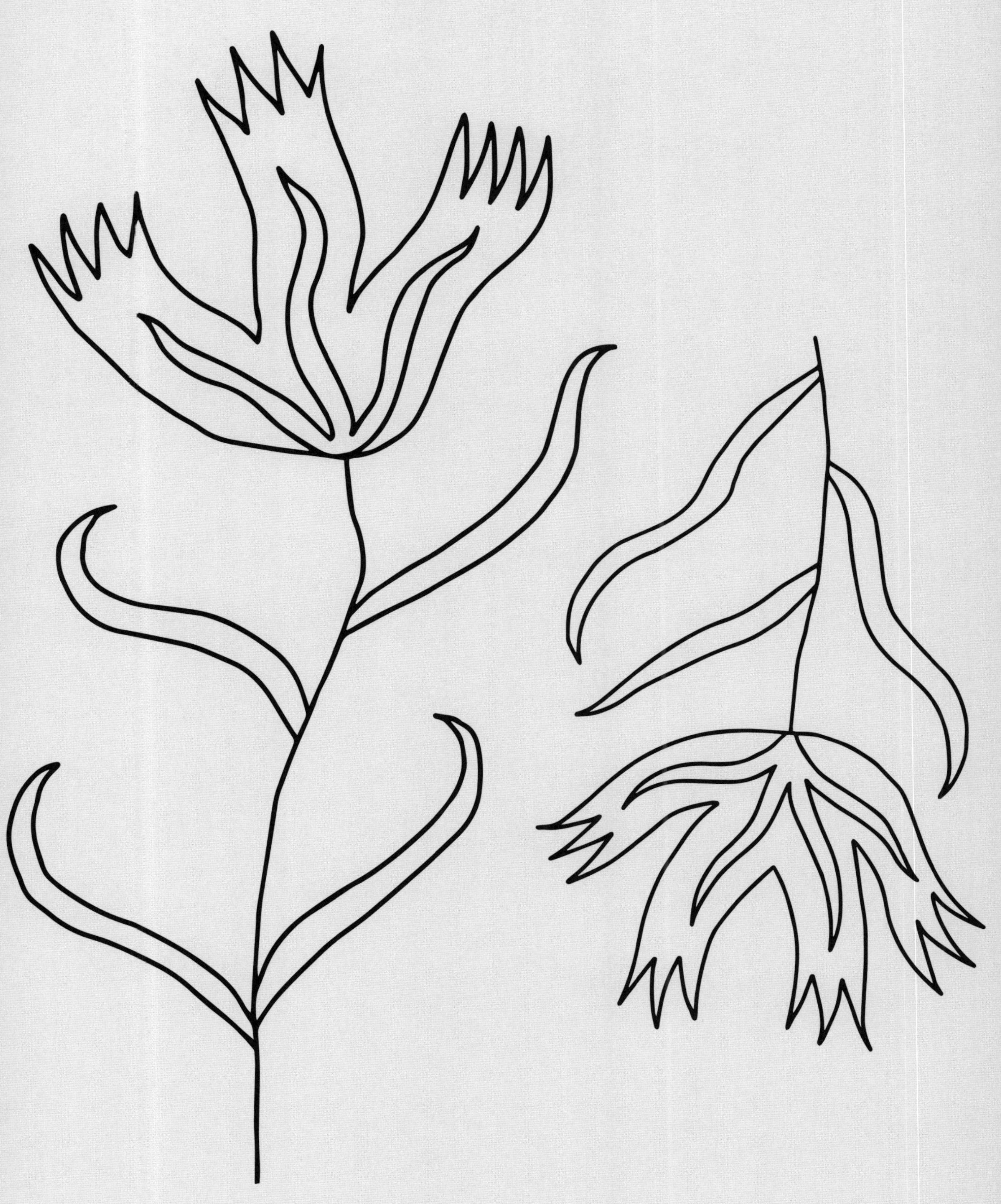

Template is at 75%. For the correct size, increase the template by 125%.

INSTRUCTIONS

1 Transfer the flower design to the garment. This simple design can easily be drawn freehand, allowing you to adapt it to the garment's shape. However, if you'd rather trace it, use your preferred transfer method (see page 134).

2 Using split stitch, create the stems of the flowers. Use green blue (# 00850) for this.

3 Fill the leaves using a slanted satin stitch. For this, I used light blue (# 00939).

4 Working with orange (# 01004), outline the flowers with split stitch.

5 Fill in the inner petals with pale pink (# 01017) using satin stitch.

6 Complete the pocket by working blanket stitch along the top edge, starting at one corner. For the blanket stitch, use orange (# 01004) and see page 61 for further guidance, if need be.

Template is at 75%. Fo
the correct size, increa
the template by 125%.

HORSE

This folk-art inspired horse design is perfect for the backs of garments. While I've used two horses in this design, you can use just one. If you prefer two, simply mirror the design for a balanced look.

LEVEL

Medium

TOOLS

- 1 x scissors
- 1 x embroidery needle
- 1 x embroidery hoop

THREAD

DMC Stranded Cotton in yellow (# 3046)
Anchor Stranded Cotton Mouliné embroidery thread in the following shades:

- Slate blue (# 00922)
- Rusty orange (# 00309)
- Light blue (# 00939)
- Green blue (# 00850)
- Orange (# 01004)

STITCHES USED IN THIS MOTIF

- Split stitch
- Satin stitch
- French knots
- Weave stitch

INSTRUCTIONS

1 Transfer the horse design to the garment using your preferred transfer method (see page 134).

2 Using split stitch, outline the shape of the horse. For this, I used slate blue (# 00922).

3 For the horse's eye, create a French knot using slate blue (# 00922). Wrap the thread around the needle three times for the French knot.

4 Fill in the horse's nose and hooves with satin stitch using yellow (# 3046) thread.

5 For the horse's tail, use split stitch to outline alternating sections. Then, fill in the remaining sections with a different colour. I used rusty orange (# 00309) and light blue (# 00939) for this.

6 Repeat the process outlined in step 5 for the horse's mane, alternating between the two colours you used for the tail.

7 Outline the horse's saddle in green blue (# 00850) using split stitch.

8 For the saddle, use weave stitch to create a basketweave effect. Start by adding vertical lines, alternating between two colours – orange (# 01004) and green blue (# 00850). Once the vertical lines are in place, weave horizontal lines using a third colour, in this case yellow (# 3046). Repeat for the second horse, if desired, remembering to reverse the motif.

FOLK ART PLANT

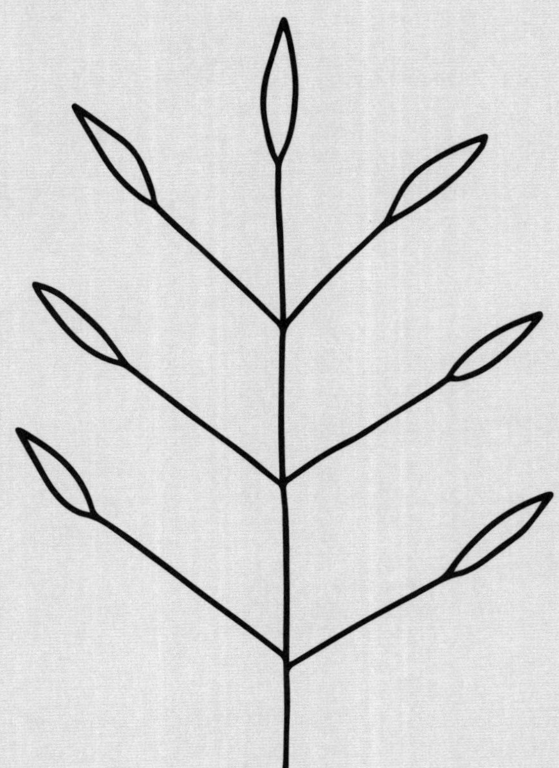

Template is at 75%. For the correct size, increase the template by 125%.

This simple plant motif is perfect for filling negative space. In the example here, I've used it to balance and complete the design with the two horses. However, you can also use this motif by itself to add a unique touch to any garment.

LEVEL

Easy

TOOLS

- 1 x scissors
- 1 x embroidery needle
- 1 x embroidery hoop

THREAD

Anchor Stranded Cotton Mouliné embroidery thread in the following shades:

- Green blue (# 00850)
- Rusty orange (# 00309)

STITCHES USED IN THIS MOTIF

- Split stitch
- Satin stitch

INSTRUCTIONS

1 Transfer the plant design to the garment using your preferred transfer method (see page 134).

2 Using split stitch, trace the centre line of the plant and then work your way along all the branches. I used green blue (# 00850) for this.

3 Using satin stitch, fill in the small leaf shapes at the end of each branch. Use rusty orange (# 00309) for the leaves.

HOW TO TRANSFER YOUR DESIGNS

For each project in this book, a black-and-white line drawing of the motifs is provided for you to use as a template. There are several methods for transferring the designs to fabric; in this section I'll walk you through two of the most commonly used options.

Please note that not all the motif templates are printed to scale because some projects are larger than the book's page dimensions. However, a downloadable PDF is available for each motif (scan the QR code below for access) and these can be resized before printing to fit your specific garment.

With any transfer method, I always recommend testing it on some scrap fabric first to ensure it washes off easily and doesn't leave any marks. Some transfer pens and chalk papers may leave a residue.

1. FREEHAND DRAWING

This is my personal favourite. When creating my designs, I prefer to draw them freehand directly onto the fabric using a water-soluble fabric pen. My go-to brand is Leonis, which comes in a pack of five pens.

To use this method, simply copy the motifs from the book by eye. After completing your embroidery, dab the fabric with a damp cloth and the pen marks will vanish, leaving a clean design.

2. TRANSFER PAPER

For those who prefer a more precise transfer method, I recommend using transfer paper. Various brands are available, but DMC offer packs containing both light and dark transfer paper, which makes it easy to transfer designs onto different fabric colours.

To Use Transfer Paper:

1. Print the to-scale motifs from the PDF or trace the designs from the book onto tracing paper.
2. Ensure the fabric is spread out on a hard, flat surface. You may wish to iron the fabric to ensure a smooth surface for transferring.
3. Place the transfer paper on the fabric with the chalky, pigmented side facing down and the fabric's right side facing up.
4. Position the printout or tracing of the motif on top of the transfer paper.
5. Using a pencil, ballpoint pen or stylus, trace over the design, applying gentle pressure. This will transfer the design to the fabric, ready for embroidery.
6. To remove the transfer lines, simply dab with a damp cloth or gently rub away with a pencil eraser.

Scan the QR code to download the motif templates.

NEXT STEPS

Now that you've completed some of the projects, you hopefully have a better understanding of how to create and execute various embroidery motifs. Why not take the next step and use your newfound knowledge to experiment with designing your own creations?

For me, designing is one of the most exciting aspects of embroidery; the possibilities are endless. Whether you're inspired by nature, architecture or something entirely abstract, there's always new subject matter to be explored.

The shape and style of the garment you're working with will often guide your design choices: if you're unsure where to start, try sketching out the garment on paper and experimenting with different design options. This will help you visualize how the embroidery will look on the piece and ensure you find a composition that you're happy with.

Once you've settled on a design, you can transfer it to the garment and start stitching. But if you're still uncertain about where to begin, the following pages outline some steps I take when I'm in need of inspiration, which you might find helpful.

DESIGN TIPS

- I often start by selecting a blank garment and choosing my thread colours before deciding on the design itself. Sometimes, the colours themselves have an influence on the motifs and shapes that emerge.
- Keep an eye out for visual elements in everyday life that inspire creativity. It could be something as simple as a flower, a tile pattern you notice on a walk or even a beautiful colour combination you spot. I recommend keeping a visual diary of sketches or taking photos on your phone of anything that catches your eye – these little details can become your next design inspiration.
- I love leafing through old books and magazines for visual inspiration. These sources can be a goldmine of ideas for unique motifs or interesting colour pairings that you might not have thought of.
- Embroidery design is all about embracing experimentation. Don't be afraid to try new things, make mistakes and refine your ideas along the way. The more you explore, the more you'll discover what truly excites you as a designer. So, gather your threads and start bringing your own ideas to life!

RESOURCES

Thread Colours

I've provided a list of the thread colours I used for the motifs alongside each project. I primarily used Anchor threads with some DMC threads included as well. If your local haberdashery carries only one brand, don't worry! You can easily match the colours across the two brands using a conversion chart, which will help you find the corresponding colour code. For converting colour codes between Anchor and DMC, simply run a search on your web browser: 'convert Anchor to DMC' or vice versa.

Online Suppliers

If you're having trouble finding the necessary supplies locally, here are some great online suppliers to help you source the materials for the projects:

DMC – dmc.com

- Six-strand cotton embroidery thread
- Transfer paper
- Embroidery hoops
- Embroidery scissors

Anchor – anchorcrafts.com

- Six-strand cotton embroidery thread

Amazon – amazon.co.uk/com or DMC – dmc.com

- Water-soluble embroidery marker pens

With these resources, you should be well equipped to follow the projects, no matter where you are!

ABOUT THE AUTHOR

Madeleine Kemsley is a textile artist and illustrator based in Cornwall, specializing in hand embroidery. Her designs reflect a harmonious blend of technical skill and an appreciation for storytelling, characterized by naïve yet intricate motifs, vibrant colours and a touch of whimsy. Her work draws inspiration from the beauty of nature, folk art and the simplicity of everyday life, creating pieces that feel timeless, yet joyful.

Madeleine has a profound love for tactile craft. She finds immense satisfaction in working with her hands; the rhythmic motions of stitching offering a tangible connection to the materials she uses. This hands-on approach allows her to immerse herself fully in her creative process, with each stitch serving as a meditative practice that brings her closer to the work at hand.

Embroidery holds a special place in Madeleine's heart. She is self-taught in this art form and first discovered its therapeutic qualities during a particularly anxious phase of her life. The act of embroidery provided a sense of calm and focus, offering her a creative outlet that was soothing. Over time, this craft became more than just a hobby – it evolved into an essential part of her life. The process of stitching, with its deliberately unhurried pace and attention to detail, allowed her to slow down and centre herself.

Madeleine's personal journey with embroidery has deeply influenced the way she approaches her work. It's not just about creating beautiful designs – it's also about sharing the therapeutic, grounding experience of the craft with others. Through her pieces, Madeleine hopes to evoke a sense of joy and comfort, inviting others to find a similar feeling of peace through the art of embroidery. Whether through the hand-embroidered works available in her shop, or her collaborations with brands, Madeleine continues to explore the intersection of artistry and mindfulness.

ACKNOWLEDGEMENTS

When I was first approached to create this book, my initial instinct was to say no, purely out of fear that I wouldn't be able to pull it off. It felt like a huge and overwhelming task and unlike anything I've worked on before. I'm so glad I decided to ignore these doubts because it has been a truly amazing project to work on, and it feels very special to be able to share the craft that brings me so much contentment.

So many people have played a significant role in helping me get to this point and in making this book a reality, and I'm deeply grateful to all of them. First and foremost, a heartfelt thank you to the team at Quadrille for trusting me with this incredible opportunity. I'm particularly thankful to Harriet for reaching out and making it all happen; to Chelsea for her guidance throughout the process; and to Alicia for her creative input on the book's design and layout.

I'd also like to acknowledge my parents for their support and encouragement as I pursued an unconventional path by choosing a creative career. I am very aware that not everyone has the privilege of such loving and fun parents, and I'm massively grateful to them.

A special thanks to everyone who supported me throughout the creation of this book. I'm not always great at managing stress, so I'm grateful (and sorry) to anyone who had to bear with me during this time – especially my partner, Ollie. I'd also like to extend my thanks to Ollie's parents, Helen and Mike, for their hospitality while I worked on a large portion of the book at their lovely house during a visit to Australia.

Finally, a massive thank you to the entire shoot team for bringing this book to life: Amelia for photographing my work so beautifully, Rosa and Emma for being such dreamy models, and Ellie for being an invaluable shoot assistant.

Quadrille, Penguin Random House UK, One Embassy Gardens, 8 Viaduct Gardens, London SW11 7BW

Quadrille Publishing Limited is part of the Penguin Random House group of companies whose addresses can be found at global.penguinrandomhouse.com

Published by Quadrille in 2025

www.penguin.co.uk

A CIP catalogue record for this book is available from the British Library

ISBN 978-1-83783-424-2
10 9 8 7 6 5 4 3 2 1

Managing Director: Sarah Lavelle
Editorial Director: Harriet Butt
Managing Editor: Chelsea Edwards
Design Manager: Katherine Case
Designer: Alicia House
Photographer, Art Direction and Producer: Amelia Pemberton
Photographer's Assistant: Ellie Kramer
Models: Rosa Lily James and Emma Scott
Hair and Makeup: Sjain McDonald
Production Controller: Sumayyah Waheed

Colour reproduction by F1

Printed in China by C&C Offset Printing Co., Ltd.

The authorised representative in the EEA is Penguin Random House Ireland, Morrison Chambers, 32 Nassau Street, Dublin D02 YH68.

Penguin Random House is committed to a sustainable future for our business, our readers and our planet. This book is made from Forest Stewardship Council® certified paper.

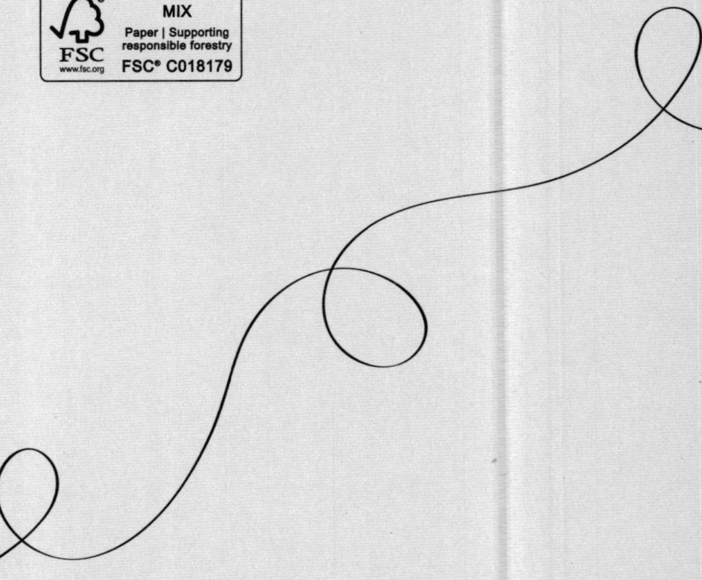